PET HEAVEN

THE ANIMAL ACCESSORY BIBLE

SALLY MUIR & JOANNA OSBORNE

PET HEAVEN
THE ANIMAL ACCESSORY BIBLE

SALLY MUIR & JOANNA OSBORNE

PHOTOGRAPHY BY DIANA MILLER

QUADRILLE

First published in 2007 by **Quadrille Publishing Limited**
Alhambra House, 27–31 Charing Cross Road, London WC2H 0LS

Editorial Director Jane O'Shea
Creative Director Helen Lewis
Project Editor Laura Herring
Designer Katherine Case
Editor and Pattern Checker Sally Harding
Pattern Checker Marilyn Wilson
Photographer Diana Miller
Photographer's Assistant Danielle Wood
Production Vincent Smith, Funsho Asemota

Text © 2007 Sally Muir and Joanna Osborne
Photography © 2007 Diana Miller
Design and layout © 2007 Quadrille Publishing Limited

Cataloguing in Publication Data:
a catalogue record for this book is available from the British Library.

ISBN 978 184400 519 2
Printed in China

CONTENTS

INTRODUCTION

At last you can stitch for your bitch, purl for your Persian, lavish your affection and skill on the pet that you love. **Pet Heaven** includes an extensive range of designs for almost every pet imaginable: hamsters, cats, horses, goldfish, birds, dogs, tortoises and more. What cat wouldn't yearn for a mouse mat to lounge on? What fourteen-year-old would not want to knit their horse a personalised blanket? Who wouldn't want to make a sophisticated and stylish tent for their tortoise to winter in, or a balaclava to protect their dog's ears from the misery of fireworks? Without spending a fortune, you can now adorn and accessorise your pet and keep them up to date with fashion.

Our patterns range from simple designs, which can be knitted by the ten-year-old beginner for their new kitten, to more complicated patterns, like the wire bird feeder, for the experienced knitter in search of an exciting challenge. The designs are meant to be practical as well as chic – they aren't intended just for dressing up your pet. And we intend these patterns to be adaptable. If you don't have a dog but like the look of the party dog collars, then why not make one for your ferret? If your pot-bellied pig would like to lounge on a dog beanbag, why not? As well as providing patterns that you can follow, we would like you to use this book as a basis to invent accessories to suit the particular foibles of your own individual pet. Use it as a source of ideas and don't feel you have to slavishly follow each pattern. We would like you to change the colours, shapes, customise it in any way you like. Pets come in a vast array of sizes and shapes so use these ideas to make your unique pet its own personalised knitted accessory. Finally, even if you don't have an animal of your own, we wouldn't want you to feel discriminated against: you can still award yourself a rosette, make a slightly larger beanbag or even knit your very own easy-care companion from our selection of knitted pets.

KNITTING BASICS

KNITTING FOR PETS

YARN SPECIFICS

The accessories in this book have been designed using Rowan and Jaeger Yarns, which are widely available throughout Europe, America and over the Internet. Visit www.knitrowan.com where you will find a full range of yarns, colours and stockists (and see pages 142–3). If you are a beginner, you can go to a local yarn shop where the (generally) helpful staff will give you all the assistance you need to track down yarns.

The majority of these pet accessories are knitted in double-knitting-weight wool yarns. If you decide to use a yarn other than the specified yarn, do remember to knit a 10cm (4in) square to check the tension and then adjust the needle size accordingly.

The number of metres (yards) per 50g (1³/₄oz) ball varies from yarn to yarn, so when using a substitute yarn, be sure to calculate the number of balls you need by the number of metres (yards) rather than by weight.

Some of the designs use oddments of several colours. These give you the opportunity to use up leftover yarns. Before beginning, however, check the yarn descriptions on page 142 to make sure that your leftovers are a good match in thickness to the main colour you are using.

TENSION

Working your knitting to the correct size is a knotty problem, especially when it involves knitting dog coats, so do knit a tension swatch. Count the number of stitches and rows to 10cm (4in) on your swatch. If your swatch has more rows or stitches than the number specified, then use knitting needles that are one size larger, and if it has fewer stitches or rows, then try one size smaller needles. Getting the number of stitches to 10cm (4in) right is more important than the number of rows, as length is generally determined by merely knitting to a specified length in centimetres (inches).

Working a tension swatch seems tedious, but it is definitely worth the time it takes, particularly if the design comes in various sizes. The swatch also gives you a chance to see how the yarn and stitch pattern knit up. Keep these swatches, and once you have collected about 20 swatches, sew them together into a blanket for your pet (see the Horse Blanket on page 54 for an example of knitted patchwork).

DOG COAT SIZES

The dog coat patterns are written for five sizes. But dogs do vary enormously in size. Here are the measurements on which we based most of our dog coats:

	Chest	Body length	Collar
Extra small	30.5cm/12in	30.5cm/12in	25.5cm/10in
Small	40.5cm/16in	35.5cm/14in	27.5cm/11in
Medium	50.5cm/20in	45.5cm/18in	33cm/13in
Large	61cm/24in	56cm/22in	38cm/15in
Extra large	66cm/26in	61cm/24in	43cm/17in

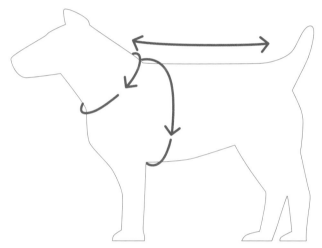

When you are measuring your dog to decide which size to knit, the most important measurement is around the widest part of the dog's chest, just behind the front legs, followed by the collar size and then the body length. For example, if your dog has a medium-sized rib cage, a small neck and a long back, it is best to opt for Medium.

It is very easy to shorten or lengthen a dog coat, and the best place is mentioned in the individual patterns.

PROTECT YOUR PETS

The most essential thing to remember when knitting for your pets is to make sure that all beads and buttons are securely sewn on – you don't want your animals to swallow them.

BASIC KNITTING TECHNIQUES

Follow these knitting instructions to learn how to knit. With these basics you can make all of the easy and intermediate patterns in this book. Or, best of all, ask an experienced knitter to show you how to knit – it is so much easier to learn when shown first hand.

For more extensive techniques, look on the Internet (try www.knitting-and-crochet-guild.org.uk or www.angelyarns.com).

CASTING ON

There are several ways of casting on, but this is the method that we prefer. It gives a more elastic edge than other techniques, which is useful when the cast-on row is followed by a garter stitch or stocking stitch fabric. Start with a slip knot – this forms the first loop of the cast-on stitches.

The slip knot

1 Wind the yarn twice around two fingers.

2 Using a knitting needle, pull the back loop through the front one to form a loop on the needle. Pull the yarn ends to tighten the loop on the needle.

The thumb cast-on

1 Make a slip knot about 1 metre (39in) from the end of the yarn. (You can alter this length in future according to the number of stitches needed.) Holding the knitting needle with the slip knot in your right hand, wind the loose end of yarn around your left thumb from front to back as shown (and leave the ball end of the yarn hanging for the time being).
2 Insert the needle under the loop on your thumb as shown.

3 Wrap the yarn coming from the ball around the tip of the needle as shown.
4 Draw the yarn around the needle through the loop on the thumb to form a stitch. For an even tension, tighten the stitch by removing your left thumb close to the right needle. Continue in this way until you have the required number of cast-on stitches.

THE KNIT STITCH

1 Hold the needle with the cast-on stitches in your left hand and the yarn coming from the ball at the back of the work. Insert the tip of the right-hand needle from left to right into the front of the first stitch on the left-hand needle.

2 Wrap the yarn over the right-hand needle as shown.

3 Draw the yarn wrapped around the right-hand needle through the stitch on the left-hand needle to make a new stitch on the right-hand needle. Slip the original stitch off the left-hand needle.

4 Continue in this way until all the stitches on the left-hand needle have been knitted and transferred onto the right-hand needle. The first row as been completed.

THE PURL STITCH

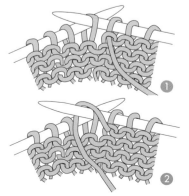

1 Hold the needle with the cast-on stitches on in your left hand and the yarn coming from the ball at the front of the work. Insert the tip of the right-hand needle from right to left into the front of the first stitch on the left-hand needle.

2 Wrap the yarn over the right-hand needle as shown.

3 Draw the yarn wrapped around the right-hand needle through the stitch on the left-hand needle to make a new stitch on the right-hand needle. Slip the original stitch off the left-hand needle.

4 Continue in this way until all the stitches on the left-hand needle have been knitted and transferred onto the right-hand needle.

BASIC STITCH PATTERNS

The basic stitch patterns in knitting are garter stitch, stocking stitch, reverse stocking stitch, ribbing and moss stitch. They are all formed by simple combinations of knit and purl stitches.

Garter stitch

If every row is worked in knit stitches, garter sittch is formed. Garter stitch fabric has a bumpy appearance. It has more rows per centimetre (inch) than stocking stitch and is reversible.

Stocking stitch

Stocking sitch is formed by working a row of knit stitches and a row of purl stitches alternately. The smooth side (the knit-stitch side) is the right side.

Reverse stocking stitch

Reverse stocking sitch is formed in exactly the same way as stocking stitch, but the knobbly side (the purl-stitch side) is the right side.

Ribbing

Ribbing is an elastic knitted fabric generally used for borders. Work alternate knit and purl stitches across the row. On the following rows all the knit stitches are knit and all the purl stitches purled to create vertical ridges.

Moss stitch

Like ribbing, moss stitch is often used for borders on knitting, but it has less elasticity. It is formed by working one knit stitch and one purl stitch alternately across the first row, then on following rows, purling each knit stitch and knitting each purl stitch.

LOOPY STITCH

There are many techniques for creating loop stitches in knitting, but this is the method used for the toy Guinea Pig's coat (see page 122). It creates secure loops approximately 2cm (³/₄in) long on the right side of the knitting.

You can work as many or as few rows as you wish in garter stitch between the loop rows, but always work the loop stitches at the back of the work on a wrong side row.

Begin the row by inserting the tip of the right needle knitwise into the first stitch on the left needle. Place the first finger of the left hand behind the stitch and wrap the yarn around the finger and the tip of right needle as shown, then knit the stitch without dropping it from the left needle. Keeping the finger inside the yarn wrap, insert the tip of the left needle from right to left through the front of the stitch just made (on the right needle) and slip this stitch back onto the left needle. Knit the slipped stitch and the next stitch on the left needle together through the back of the loops (k2tog tbl). Now slide the finger out of the loop. This completes the first loop stitch. Work every stitch in the same way to the end of the row.

CASTING OFF

When your knitting is finished, you cast off the remaining stitches. It is important to always work the stitches in the pattern stitch used. For example, if the cast-off row follows a purl row in a stocking stitch fabric, work a knitwise cast-off as shown below.

1 For a knitwise cast-off, begin by knitting the first two stitches. Then using the left-hand needle, lift the first stitch over the second stitch and drop it off the right-hand needle. Knit the next stitch and repeat.

2 Continue to do this until one stitch remains on the right-hand needle. Slip this remaining stitch off the needle, break off the yarn, pass the yarn end through the loop and pull tightly to secure.

For a purlwise cast-off, repeat as above but working in purl stitches.

INCREASING

When knitting some of the accessories in this book, you may need to use one of these two increasing methods. Each one has a particular purpose.

Working into the front and back of a stitch
(known as 'inc 1')
This increase is usually used when a single increase is needed at the beginning and the end of a row.

Knit into the stitch and before slipping it off the left-hand needle, knit into the back of the same stitch as shown to make an extra stitch.

Yarn forward
(known as 'yfwd')
This increase method is used in lace stitch patterns (and for buttonholes) because it creates a visible hole in the knitted fabric.

On a knit row, bring the yarn to the front of the work between the two needles, then take it over the right-hand needle to the back of the work and knit the next stitch in the usual way as shown. This creates an extra loop on the right-hand needle.

DECREASING

The two methods for decreasing used in this book are the simple decrease and the slip-stitch decrease.

Simple decrease

(known as 'k2tog' or 'p2tog')

On a knit row, insert the right-hand needle into two stitches and knit them together as one stitch as shown. On a purl row, purl the two stitches together.

Slip-stitch decrease

(known as 'sl 1, k1, psso')

1 Slip the next stitch onto the right-hand needle *(sl 1)*, then knit the next stitch *(k1)*.

2 Pass the slipped stitch over the knit stitch and let it drop off the right-hand needle *(psso)*.

JOINING IN NEW YARN

If you need to join in a new ball of yarn, it is much easier to start it at the beginning of a new row. If you are knitting stripes, however, do not cut off the yarn every time you change colours. Instead, drop the yarn at the side of the knitting and pick it up again when you need the same colour again. (This only works when the stripes have an even number of rows.)

COLOUR KNITTING

There are two main techniques for working with more than one colour in the same row of knitting – the intarsia technique and the stranding (or Fair Isle) technique.

Intarsia technique

This method is used when knitting individual, large blocks of colour. It is best to a use small ball (or long length) for each area of colour, otherwise the yarns will easily become tangled.

Follow the chart for the colour pattern, and when changing to the new colour, twist the yarns on the wrong side of the work to prevent holes forming.

When starting a new row, turn the knitting so that the yarns that are hanging from the knitting untwist as much as possible. You may occasionally have to reorganise the yarns at the back of the knitting.

Your work may look a little messy but don't be concerned; once the ends are all sewn in and the work is pressed, it will look very impressive.

Stranding (or Fair Isle) technique

If a pattern is repeated in small blocks of colour (no more than 4 stitches) across the entire row, you can use the stranding (or Fair Isle) technique.

Begin knitting with the first colour, then drop this when you introduce the second colour. Strand the first colour across the back of the second colour. When you come to the first colour again, take it under the second colour to twist the yarns. When you come to the second colour again, take it over the first colour. The secret of this method is not to pull the strands on the wrong side of the work too tightly, otherwise the work will pucker.

MATTRESS STITCH

Mattress stitch is the neatest of all the methods used for sewing seams and can be used on any type of seam. As it is worked on the right side of the knitting, it is particularly suited to projects where you need a flat seam and for when you want patterns or stripes to match up – for example, on the Hamster House, the Dog Coats, Cat Cushions and the Beanbags. For the best finish, work this stitch one stitch in from the edge of the knitting.

1 With the right sides of the knitting facing you, secure the yarn at the bottom of the seam. Take the yarn to the opposite side, insert the needle under two bars between the first and second stitches and pull the needle through to the front. Repeat this on the opposite side, drawing the edges closely together, but not so tight that the knitting gathers. Continue in the same way.

OVERCAST STITCH/WHIP STITCH

This stitch can be used if you need a flat seam – for example, on the Horse Blanket and Bird Feeder.

With the right sides together, secure the yarn at the beginning of the seam. Then take the needle over the top of the two edges and from back to front through both layers, close to the edge. Repeat, keeping the stitches slanted at the same angle and evenly spaced. Once pressed this should give a flat seam.

BACKSTITCH

Backstitch is a handy and firm standby stitch for sewing seams on knitting.

With right sides together, pin and then secure the yarn at the right-hand end. Working over one knitted stitch at a time, bring the needle to the front of the knitting, take it forward and through the knitting to the back. Then take it along one knitted stitch and out to the front, and then return to the end of the first stitch and through to the back. As with learning to knit, the easiest way to learn this is to watch someone else doing it.

BLANKET STITCH

Blanket stitch is used to give a fabric a finished edge – for example, for the Silhouette Dog Coat. Unlike the previous hand stitches, this stitch is sewn to be seen.

Secure a contrasting yarn to the edge of the knitting. Bring the needle up from the wrong side of the knitting, about 5mm ($\frac{1}{4}$in) in from the edge, making a diagonal stitch. When you make the next stitch, 5mm ($\frac{1}{4}$in) away from the last stitch, take the needle through the loop formed and pull down to make a right angle at the edge of the knitting.

FINISHING TECHNIQUES

Finishing your knitting is an essential moment. You can either produce a perfectly finished accessory or ruin a beautifully knitted accessory.

WEAVING IN THE LOOSE YARN ENDS

Using a large tapestry needle with a blunt point (or a yarn needle), darn the loose ends into the back of the work and cut off.

When sewing in ends on intarsia-work, weave them through the back of the same colour.

PRESSING

Press all the knitted pieces before sewing seams unless your instructions state otherwise. The yarn label will give you precise pressing and care instructions for that particular yarn, but here are a few hints:

• Cover the knitting with a clean, damp cloth and press ligthly with a steam iron. Do not drag the iron over the knitting, but instead lift it gently up and down.
• Press stocking stitch and especially intarsia-work more firmly, blocking if necessary.
• Press ribbing extremely lightly or avoid (you do not want to flatten it as it will loose its spring).
• Garter stitch needs only a very light pressing or none at all.

KNITTING REMEDIES

Occasionally, when knitting, minor disasters occur. Here are two handy knitting remedies.

PICKING UP DROPPED STITCHES

If a stitch drops off the needle, you can usually pick it up with the tip of the other needle and pop it back on. If the stitch has dropped down several rows and formed a ladder, however, you will need to use a crochet hook.

Working from the front of the work, insert the hook into the centre of dropped stitch, pick up the next bar between two stitches and draw it through to form a new stitch. Repeat this until you reach the row you are working on.

DARNING HOLES

Darning is a very useful skill to learn, although almost impossible to perfect. Animals, perhaps, won't look after your beautifully made accessories as you would like them to, so the odd hole will appear here or there. It is far better to repair any holes than to leave them to get bigger.

Try to find some yarn to roughly match the accessory. If it is too thick, you can untwist it and separate the strands to make it finer. Using a blunt-ended tapestry or yarn needle, loosely stitch from one side of the hole to the other – you are making a 'mesh base' to weave through. The idea of darning is to replace the hole in the knitting, so do not pull the sides of the hole together.

Once you have a 'mesh base', weave the yarn in and out. Continue until the repair is as firm and secure as possible.

CUSTOMISING YOUR KNITS

DESIGNING MOTIFS ON GRAPH PAPER

If you want to create a unique motif for your pet's accessory – your horse's favourite food for the blanket, your dog's favourite toy on his coat, your lucky number on the Football Strip, for instance – use this method:

Purchase a large sheet of graph paper from an art or stationery shop. Bear in mind that there are generally more stitches than rows per cm/inch so you will need to elongate your object when you draw it onto the paper. (If you like, you can download graph paper tailored to your tension at: www.thedietdiary.com.) Copy the image that you want to use onto the graph paper. Each square of the graph paper will represent one stitch so simply colour in the squares depending on what colour yarn you would like to use. Now you can get on with customising your pet's accessory.

ALPHABET

We have included an alphabet for you to use if you want to knit your pet's name, as on the Horse Blanket. You can also use it on a dog coat, cat cushion or anywhere else you wish. See page 140.

KNITTING ABBREVIATIONS

The following are the abbreviations used in this book. Special abbreviations are given with individual patterns.

alt	alternate
beg	begin(ning)
cm	centimetre(s)
cont	continu(e)(ing)
dec	decreas(e)(ing)
DK	double knitting (a lightweight to medium-weight yarn)
foll	follow(s)(ing)
g	gram(s)
in	inch(es)
inc	increas(e)(ing)
k	knit
k2tog	knit next 2 sts together
m	metre(s)
MC	main colour (of yarn)
mm	millimetre(s)
oz	ounce(s)
p	purl
p2tog	purl next 2 sts together
patt	pattern
psso	pass slipped stitch over
rem	remain(s)(ing)
rep	repeat(s)(ing)
rev st st	reverse stocking stitch; purl sts on RS rows and knit sts on WS rows

RS	right side
sl	slip
st(s)	stitch(es)
st st	stocking stitch; knit sts on RS rows and purl sts on WS rows
tog	together
WS	wrong side
yfwd	yarn forward; bring yarn to front of work between two needles and then over right-hand needle to back, to make a new stitch
yon	yarn over needle; yarn over right-hand needle to make a new stitch
*	Repeat instructions after asterisk or between asterisks as many times as instructed.
[ ]	Repeat instructions inside square brackets as many times as instructed
-	Where a hyphen appears instead of a number, it means that instructions do not apply to that size

DIFFICULTY RATING (shown at start of pattern)

Easy

Intermediate

Difficult

THE PROJECTS

BEANBAGS FOR **CAT** OR **DOG**

A cocooning, comfortable beanbag for your pet
to relax into that will look enchanting in any living
room. Blend the colours to go with your pet or house.
The beanbag comes in three sizes designed for cats
and dogs – or any stray animal that wants to curl up.

BEANBAGS FOR **CAT** OR **DOG**

LEVEL
Knitted beanbag cover: Easy
Beanbag fabric cushion: Intermediate

SIZES
Choose your size as follows:
Small – for a cat
Medium – for a small/medium dog
Large – for a large dog

The finished beanbag measures approximately 55 (62.5: 70)cm/ 22 (25: 28)in in diameter across the circular base and each of the four top segments (which form the top and sides of the bag) measures 43 (55.5: 68.5)cm/17 (22: 27)in from the cast-on edge to the tip at the centre of the beanbag.

MATERIALS
Knitted beanbag cover
Approximately 650 (750: 850)g/22$\frac{3}{4}$ (26$\frac{1}{4}$: 29$\frac{3}{4}$)oz of a selection of balls of Rowan *Scottish Tweed Aran*, Rowan *Pure Wool DK* and Jaeger *Matchmaker Merino DK* in a total of 10–13 different colours (see the Special Yarn Note on page 24)
Small amount of Jaeger *Fur* (optional)
Pair of 5.5mm (US size 9) knitting needles
4 large press studs
Beanbag cushion
Newspaper, or other large sheets of paper, for paper pattern
Approximately 2 (2.2: 2.5)m/2$\frac{1}{4}$ (2$\frac{1}{2}$: 2$\frac{3}{4}$)yd of 112cm/45in wide calico or other cotton fabric remnant and matching sewing thread
45cm/18in zipper
500g/18oz of polystyrene balls, for cushion filling

TENSION
16 sts and 30 rows to 10cm/4in measured over garter stitch using 5.5mm (US size 9) needles and Rowan *Scottish Tweed Aran*.

ABBREVIATIONS
See page 17.

SPECIAL YARN NOTE

Use the Rowan *Scottish Tweed Aran* yarn **single** when knitting the beanbag, but use the Rowan *Pure Wool DK* or Jaeger *Matchmaker Merino DK* **double**. Use Jaeger *Fur* sparingly, introducing it across only one or two rows in the top segments of the beanbag.

The yarns specified are only suggestions, as this project provides an ideal opportunity for you to use up leftover yarns in a variety of textures – the more textured the beanbag, the more interesting it will be. Remember to use your leftover aran-weight yarn single, your leftover double-knitting-weight yarn double, and very thick yarns (like the Jaeger *Fur*) only in a couple of rows. Prepare the yarn as explained before beginning your knitting.

KNITTED BEANBAG COVER

PREPARE THE YARN

Cut the aran-weight yarn into varying lengths – approximately 30.5cm/12in to 92cm/36in long. Cut the double-knitting-weight yarn to twice this length. Fold the double-knitting weight yarns in half so that they are double (see the Special Yarn Note, above), then knot the lengths together, end to end, introducing the colours randomly. (To reduce the number of knots, you can link the doubled yarn together at the fold where possible.)

Note: When you are knitting, try to position the knots on the wrong side of the work. If the occasional knot does pop through onto the right side, it is easy to push it back to the wrong side when you reach it on the next row.

BASE PIECES (MAKE 2)

With 5.5mm (US size 9) needles and prepared yarn, cast on 88 (100: 112) sts. Mark 14th (20th: 26th) cast-on st and 74th (80th: 86th) cast-on st with a coloured thread to show position of opening on base of beanbag.
Work 20 rows in garter st (knit every row). Cont in garter st throughout, dec 1 st at each end of next row and then at each end of every foll alt row 28 (30: 32) times in all. (*32 (40: 48) sts.*)
Dec 1 st at each end of next 6 (10: 14) rows.
Cast off rem 20 sts knitwise.
Make second base piece in same way.

TOP SEGMENTS (MAKE 4)

With 5.5mm (US size 9) needles, cast 74 (80: 86) sts.
Work 40 (70: 100) rows in garter st (knit every row).
Cont in garter st throughout, dec 1 st at each end of next row and then at each end of every foll 3rd row 26 (29: 32) times in all. (*22 sts.*)
Next row *K2tog, k3; rep from * to last 2 sts, k2tog. (*17 sts.*)

Work 2 rows in garter st.
Next row *K2tog, k2; rep from * to last 5 sts, k2tog, k1, k2tog. (*12 sts.*)
Work 2 rows in garter st.
Next row K2tog, k1, [k2tog] 3 times, k1, k2tog. (*7 sts.*)
Work 2 rows in garter st.
Next row K2tog, k3tog, k2tog. (*3 sts.*)
Work 1 row in garter st.
Next row K3tog, break off yarn, thread tail end through rem st and pull tight to fasten off.

TO FINISH

Darn in all yarn ends and push all knots on right side through to wrong side. Press all pieces lightly on wrong side, following instructions on yarn label.
Using a single strand of a double-knitting-weight yarn, sew pieces together as follows:
With right sides together, sew two base pieces together along cast-on edges, stitching from side edges to markers (leaving a large opening between markers for inserting cushion). Remove markers.
Sew together four top segments, stitching from tips (which are at centre of cover) to cast-on edge.
Sew cast-on edge of top to base, aligning seams on base with two of segment seams.
Sew four large press studs, equally spaced apart, to opening.

BEANBAG CUSHION

PAPER PATTERN PIECES

Use newspaper or other large sheets of paper to make the paper pattern for the cushion. (The cushion is circular, and once inserted in the knitted cover, it gives the beanbag its circular shape.)

Pattern piece for circular base

Cut a paper rectangle 29 (33: 36.5)cm/11$\frac{1}{2}$ (13: 14$\frac{1}{2}$)in by 58 (66: 73)cm/23 (26: 29)in.
Fold the rectangle in half to make a square. Using a homemade compass and measuring from one of the corners at the fold, mark 29 (33: 36.5)cm/11$\frac{1}{2}$ (13: 14$\frac{1}{2}$)in from this corner and in a curve from the adjacent corner across the square to the opposite corner. Keeping the paper folded, cut along the marked curve, then open out the semi-circle. (This finished pattern piece includes the seam allowance along the curved edge, but not along the straight edge.) Mark the position for the 45cm/18in zipper at the centre of the straight edge of the semi-circle.

Pattern piece for top segments

Cut a paper rectangle 46 (52: 58)cm/18 (20$\frac{1}{2}$: 23)in by 43 (55.5: 68.5)cm/17 (22: 27)in.
Then shape this rectangle into the shape of one of the four top segments of the cushion as follows:

Lay the rectangle with an edge 46 (52: 58)cm/18 (20.5: 23)in long at the bottom – this edge is the base of the segment.
Measure up from the base 12.5 (17.5: 22.5)cm/5 (7: 9)in along both the right and left side edge of the rectangle and make a mark.
Find the centre of the top edge of the rectangle (you can fold the rectangle in half to find the centre) and mark. Then draw a gentle curve from the centre of the top of the rectangle to each of the marks made at the side edges.
Cut along the curves. (This finished pattern piece does not include seam allowances.)

TO CUT FABRIC PIECES

Using the pattern for the base, cut two base pieces from the fabric, adding an extra 1.5cm/$\frac{1}{2}$in along the straight edge of the paper pattern for the seam allowance at the centre of the cushion. Mark the position for the zipper on each of these pieces. Using the pattern for the top segments, cut four top segments from the fabric, adding an extra 1.5cm/$\frac{1}{2}$in all around the paper pattern for the seam allowance.

TO SEW THE CUSHION

Pin the two base pieces together along the straight edges, with right sides together. Taking a 1.5cm/$\frac{1}{2}$in seam allowance throughout, stitch the seam, leaving a

45cm/18in opening for the zipper as marked. Press the seam open and press 1.5cm/$\frac{1}{2}$in to the wrong side along the zipper opening. Stitch the zipper in place and set the cushion base aside.
With right sides together, pin two top segments together along one curved edge, and stitch. Stitch the two remaining top segments together in the same way. Pin the two halves of the top together and stitch, to make a large cone shape.
Open the zipper, then pin the cone-shaped top to the base, with right sides together and aligning the base seams with two of the top segments seams (ease in the top as necessary to fit the base). Stitch along this seam twice (for strength).
Clip the seam allowances around the curves as necessary, so that the seams lie flat. Press.
Turn right side out. Fill the cushion with polystyrene balls until it is about one third full and zip the opening closed.
Insert the cushion in the knitted beanbag cover and snap closed.

CARROT CURTAIN

Why should your poor rabbit languish with almost no interior decoration in its hutch? You can now show you care by giving its home a makeover with these easy to knit and cheery curtains. If you don't have a rabbit but have a pet guinea pig instead, you can always substitute the carrots for something that guinea pigs like – dandelion leaves, green peppers, cow parsley, grass…

CARROT CURTAIN

LEVEL
Intermediate

SIZE
The finished carrot curtain measures approximately 35.5cm/14in wide by 32cm/12¹/₂in long.

Note: The curtain can be made wider or longer to fit your hutch by adding more stitches or rows.

MATERIALS
2 x 50g/1³/₄oz balls of Rowan *Pure Wool DK* in main colour **MC** (dark grey/Anthracite 003), for background
1 x 50g/1³/₄oz ball of Rowan *Pure Wool DK* in **A** (orange/Quarry 035), for carrots
1 x 25g/ ⁷/₈oz ball of Rowan *Kidsilk Haze* in **B** (green/Jelly 597), for carrot stalks
Pair of 4mm (US size 6) knitting needles
Wooden dowelling, 43cm/17in long by 6mm/¹/₄in in diameter, for curtain pole
2 screw-in metal cuphooks, for attaching dowelling to front of hutch

TENSION
22 sts and 30 rows to 10cm/4in measured over st st using 4mm (US size 6) needles and MC.

ABBREVIATIONS
See page 17.

CHART NOTE
The background in the centre of the curtain is worked in reverse stocking stitch and the carrot motifs in stocking stitch. There is a 5-stitch moss stitch border along each side edge of the curtain centre to form firm edges.
When working from the chart, read odd-numbered rows (right-side rows) from right to left, and even-numbered rows (wrong-side rows) from left to right.
When working the carrot motifs, use the intarsia method (see page 14), knitting with a separate small ball (or long length) of yarn for each area of colour and twisting yarns together on wrong side when changing colour to avoid holes. The carrot stalks are knitted separately and sewn onto the completed curtain.

TO MAKE CURTAIN
With 4mm (US size 6) needles and MC, cast on 83 sts.
Work lower border in moss st as follows:
1st moss st row (RS) K1, *p1, k1; rep from * to end.
(Last row is repeated to form moss st.)
Work 9 rows more in moss st, ending with a WS row.
Set patt for centre as follows:
1st patt row (RS) K1, [p1, k1] twice, p to last 5 sts, [k1, p1] twice, k1.
2nd patt row K1, [p1, k1] twice, K to last 5 sts, [k1, p1] twice, k1.
Rep last 2 rows once more, ending

with a WS row.
Using MC and A as required, position carrot motifs (see page 126) on next 2 rows (chart rows 5 and 6) as follows:
Next row (RS) Using MC k1, [p1, k1] twice, p8, *using A k1, using MC p13; rep from * 3 times more, using A k1, using MC p8, [k1, p1] twice, k1.
Next row Using MC k1, [p1, k1] twice, k8, *using A p1, using MC k13; rep from * 3 times more, using A p1, using MC k8, [k1, p1] twice, k1.
Cont as set, keeping 5-st side borders in moss st and following chart for 73 centre sts (working carrot motifs in st st and A, and background in rev st st and MC) until all 78 chart rows have been completed, ending with a WS row.
Break off A.
Rep 1st and 2nd patt rows 5 times, ending with a WS row.
Next row (RS) Rep 2nd patt row (to form a p-st ridge on WS).
Rep 2nd patt row once more.
Rep 1st and 2nd patt rows 4 times more.
Cast off in patt.

CARROT STALKS (MAKE 14)
With 4mm (US size 6) needles and B, cast on 15 sts.
Cast off 15 sts knitwise.
Make 13 more carrot stalks in same way.

TO FINISH
Block and press curtain lightly on wrong side, following instructions on yarn label.
Fold each stalk into a V-shape as shown, and sew one to top of each of 14 carrot motifs on curtain, using B.
Fold cast-off edge at top of curtain to wrong side and slip stitch cast-off edge to ridge row to form a channel at top of curtain. Insert curtain pole into channel. Screw two metal cuphooks to hutch, and slide curtain pole in place on hooks.

DOG COATS

We have designed a range of coats to suit your dog's every whim. The Football Strip will give your dog a sense of purpose when playing with a ball. In an equally manly vein, there is the simple, timelessly elegant Cable Coat. One of our most practical garments, it has a masculine Sean Connery feel combined with contemporary retro chic. As we all know, spots never go out of fashion, and any dog wearing the Britart-inspired Spot Dog Coat will feel equally at home in Hyde Park or Hoxton Square. Finally, ravishing yet practical, the Floral Dog Coat is for the dog who wants to stand out from the crowd. For an extravagant occasion team it with the Floral Party Dog Collar on page 66.

FOOTBALL STRIP **DOG** COAT

LEVEL
Intermediate

SIZES
See page 10 for dog measurements and sizes.

FINISHED COAT MEASUREMENTS

	Width of coat	Length to neck shaping
Extra small	35.5cm/14in	30.5cm/12in
Small	40cm/15¾in	35.5cm/14in
Medium	47cm/18½in	45.5cm/18in
Large	61cm/24in	55.5cm/22in
Extra large	67cm/26½in	61cm/24in

MATERIALS
2 (2: 3: 4: 5) x 50g/1¾oz balls of Jaeger *Matchmaker Merino DK* in main colour **MC**
1 x 50g/1¾oz ball of Jaeger *Matchmaker Merino DK* in a contrasting colour **A**
Pair of 3.25mm (US size 3) knitting needles
Pair of 4mm (US size 6) knitting needles
Set of four 3.25mm (US size 3) double-pointed knitting needles

TENSION
22 sts and 30 rows to 10cm/4in measured over st st using 4mm (US size 6) knitting needles.

ABBREVIATIONS
See page 17.

CHART NOTE
The charts are worked in st st.
When working from the charts, read odd-numbered rows (k rows) from right to left, and even-numbered rows (p rows) from left to right.
When working the chart patterns, use the intarsia method (see page 14), knitting with a separate small ball (or long length) of yarn for each area of colour and twisting yarns together on wrong side when changing colour to avoid holes.

TOP OF COAT
With 3.25mm (US size 3) needles and

MC, cast on 42 (46: 56: 76: 86) sts.
1st rib row (RS) *K1, p1; rep from * to end.
(Last row is repeated to form k1, p1 rib patt.)
Work 3 rows more in rib, ending with a WS row.
Change to A and work 2 rows more in rib.
Break off A.
Cont with MC only, work 4 rows more in rib.
Change to 4mm (US size 6) needles.
Beg st st with rib borders as follows:
Next row (RS) [K1, p1] twice, k into front and back of next st, k to last 5 sts, k into

front and back of next st, [k1, p1] twice.
Next row Rib 4 sts as set, p to last 4 sts, rib 4 sts as set.
Rep last 2 rows 7 (9: 9: 11: 11) times, ending with a WS row.
(58 (66: 76: 100: 110) sts.)

Extra Small and Small only
Cont in st st only, set position of number chart (see page 126) as follows:
Next row (RS) K27 (31: -: -: -)MC, k5A, k26 (30: -: -: -)MC.
Next row P24 (28: -: -: -)MC, p10A, p24 (28: -: -: -)MC.

Medium, Large and Extra Large only

Work straight as set, with st st at centre and 4-st rib border along each side edge, until work measures - (-: 14: 17.5: 20)cm/ - (-: 5½: 7: 8)in from cast-on edge (measuring up centre of panel), ending with a WS row.

Set position of number chart (see page 126) as follows:

Next row (RS) Rib 4 sts in MC, k- (-: 32: 44: 49)MC, k5A, k- (-: 31: 43: 48)MC, rib 4 sts in MC.

Next row Rib 4 sts in MC, p- (-: 29: 41: 46)MC, p10A, p- (-: 29: 41: 46)MC, rib 4 sts in MC.

Cont foll chart as set and working 4-st rib borders until work measures - (-: 15: 20: 22.5)cm/- (-: 6: 8: 9)in from cast-on edge, ending with a WS row.

All sizes

Beg with a k row, work all sts in st st and cont foll chart until all 40 chart rows have been completed (then cont with MC only) **and at the same time** cont in patt as now set until work measures 14 (17.5: 28: 33: 35.5)cm/5½ (7 :11: 13: 14)in from cast-on edge, ending with a p row.

(**Note:** If required, increase or reduce length of coat here and match this change on gusset.)

Mark for leg openings

Mark each end of last row with a coloured thread to indicate beg of leg openings. Cont in st st until work measures 20 (25.5: 35.5: 40.5: 44.5)cm/ 8 (10: 14: 16: 17½)in from cast-on edge, ending with a p row.

Mark each end of last row with a coloured thread to indicate end of leg openings. Cont in st st until work measures 25.5 (30.5: 40.5: 45.5: 50.5)cm/ 10 (12: 16: 18: 20)in, ending with a p row.

Next row (RS) K8 (10: 12: 18: 20), k2tog, k to last 10 (12: 14: 20: 22) sts, k2tog, k8 (10: 12: 18: 20).

Purl 1 row.

Rep last 2 rows row 5 (7: 8: 14: 14) times. (46 (50: 58: 70: 80) sts.)

Work straight in st st until work measures 30.5 (35.5: 45.5: 55.5: 61)cm/ 12 (14: 18: 22: 24)in from cast-on

edge, ending with a p row.

Break off yarn and leave sts on a st holder.

GUSSET

With 3.25mm (US size 3) needles and MC, cast on 16 (22: 28: 34: 38) sts. Work 4 rows in k1, p1 rib as for top of coat.

Change to A and work 2 rows more in rib.

Break off A.

Cont with MC only, work 2 rows more in rib.

Change to 4mm (US size 6) needles.

Beg with a k row, work in st st until gusset measures 6.5 (7.5: 13: 13: 13)cm/ 3½ (3: 5: 5: 5)in from cast-on edge, ending with a p row.

Mark for leg openings

Mark each end of last row with a coloured thread to indicate beg of leg openings. Cont in st st throughout, work until leg openings measure same as leg openings on top of coat, ending with a p row. Mark each end of last row with a coloured thread to indicate end of leg openings. Work until gusset measures 15 (17.5: 22.5: 25: 30.5)cm/6 (7: 9: 10: 12)in from cast-on edge, ending with a p row. Set position of badge chart (see page 126) as follows:

Next row (RS) K7 (10: 13: 16: 18)MC, k1A, k8 (11: 14: 17: 19)MC.

Next row P7 (10: 13: 16: 18)MC, p3A, p6 (9: 12: 15: 17)MC.

Cont in st st foll chart as set until chart row 20 has been completed (then cont with MC only) **and at the same time** cont as set until work measures 20 (21.5: 26.5: 25: 30.5)cm/8 (8½: 10½: 10: 12)in from cast-on edge, ending with a p row.

Dec 1 st at each end of next 4 (6: 9: 11: 12) rows, ending with a p (p: k: k: p) row. (8 (10: 10: 12: 14) sts.)

Work straight until gusset measures 23 (25.5: 30.5: 35.5: 38.5)cm/ 9 (10: 12: 14: 15)in from cast-on edge, ending with a p row.

Break off yarn and leave first 4 (5: 5: 6: 7) sts on one st holder and rem 4 (5: 5: 6: 7) sts on another st holder.

TO FINISH

Press top of coat and gusset lightly on wrong side, following instructions on yarn label and avoiding ribbing.

With right sides together and matching leg-opening markers, sew gusset to top of coat, leaving seam open between markers for front-leg openings. Turn coat right side out.

Collar

The collar is worked so that it is divided at the centre front (under the chin) after 4 rows in rib.

With RS facing and using set of four 3.25mm (US size 3) double-pointed needles and A, k 4 (5: 5: 6: 7) sts from left gusset st holder, k 46 (50: 58: 70: 80) sts from top-of-coat st holder and k4 (5: 5: 6: 7) sts from right gusset st holder (distributing sts evenly on 3 needles and knitting with 4th needle).

(54 (60: 68: 82: 94) sts.)

Work 4 rounds in k1, p1 rib, ending at centre front.

Now turn work and start working collar back and forth in rows of garter st (knit every row) so that it is divided at centre front as follows:

Next row (RS of collar) K13 (15: 17: 20: 23), k into front and back of next st, k to last 14 (16: 18: 21: 24) sts, k into front and back of next st, k13 (15: 17: 20: 23).

Next row (WS of collar) K to end.

Rep last 2 rows 7 times, ending with a WS row.

Change to MC and knit 2 rows.

Break off MC.

Change to A and knit 4 rows.

Cast off knitwise.

Edging on front leg openings

With RS facing and using set of four 3.25mm (US size 3) double-pointed needles and A, pick up and knit 30 (38: 38: 46: 46) sts around one front leg opening.

Work 6 rounds in k1, p1 rib.

Change to MC and work 1 round more in rib.

Break off MC.

Change to A and work 2 rounds more in rib.

Cast off loosely in rib.

CABLE **DOG** COAT

LEVEL
Easy

SIZES
See page 10 for dog measurements and sizes.

FINISHED COAT MEASUREMENTS

	Width of coat	Length to neck shaping
Extra small	31cm/12$\frac{1}{4}$in	30.5cm/12in
Small	37.5cm/14$\frac{3}{4}$in	35.5cm/14in
Medium	45cm/17$\frac{3}{4}$in	45.5cm/18in
Large	58.5cm/23in	55.5cm/22in
Extra large	65cm/25$\frac{1}{2}$in	61cm/24in

MATERIALS
2 (2: 2: 3: 4) x 50g/1$\frac{3}{4}$oz balls of Rowan *Felted Tweed*
Pair of 3.25mm (US size 3) knitting needles
Pair of 4mm (US size 6) knitting needles
Short double-pointed 4mm (US size 6) knitting needle or cable needle

TENSION
22 sts and 30 rows to 10cm/4in measured over st st using 4mm (US size 6) needles.
14-stitch cable panel measures approximately 4cm/1$\frac{1}{2}$in wide.

ABBREVIATIONS
C10B = slip next 5 sts onto cable needle and hold at back of work, k5, then k5 from cable needle.
See page 17

TOP OF COAT
With 3.25mm (US size 3) needles, cast on 42 (46: 56: 76: 86) sts.
1st rib row *K1, p1; rep from * to end. (Last row is repeated to form k1, p1 rib patt.)
Work 5 rows more in rib.
Change to 4mm (US size 6) needles.
Beg cable patt as follows:
1st patt row (RS) [K1, p1] twice, k into front and back of next st, k9 (11: 16: 26: 31); for cable panel, work p2, k10, p2; k9 (11: 16: 26: 31), k into front and back of next st, [k1, p1] twice.
(44 (48: 58: 78: 88) sts.)

2nd patt row [K1, p1] twice, p11 (13: 18: 28: 33); for cable panel, work k2, p10, k2; p11 (13: 18: 28: 33), [k1, p1] twice.
3rd patt row [K1, p1] twice, k into front and back of next st, k10 (12: 17: 27: 32); for cable panel, work p2, k10, p2; k10 (12: 17: 27: 32), k into front and back of next st, [k1, p1] twice.
(46 (50: 60: 80: 90) sts.)
4th patt row [K1, p1] twice, p12 (14: 19: 29: 34); for cable panel, work k2, p10, k2; p12 (14: 19: 29: 34), [k1, p1] twice.
5th patt row [K1, p1] twice, k into front and back of next st, k11 (13: 18: 28:

33); for cable panel, work p2, k10, p2; k11 (13: 18: 28: 33), k into front and back of next st, [k1, p1] twice.
(48 (52: 62: 82: 92) sts.)
6th patt row [K1, p1] twice, p13 (15: 20: 30: 35); for cable panel, work k2, p10, k2; p13 (15: 20: 30: 35), [k1, p1] twice.
7th patt row [K1, p1] twice, k into front and back of next st, k12 (14: 19: 29: 34); for cable panel, work p2, C10B, p2; k12 (14: 19: 29: 34), k into front and back of next st, [k1, p1] twice.
(50 (54: 64: 84: 94) sts.)
This sets patt with st st at each side of a

central 14-st cable panel and a 4-st rib border along each side edge.

Cont in patt as set, crossing cable (as in 7th patt row) on every foll 10th row, **and at the same time** cont to inc 1 st at each end (inside rib borders) of 4 (6: 6: 8: 8) foll alt rows (RS rows), ending with a RS row. (58 (66: 76: 100: 110) sts.)

Work straight in patt as set until cable panel measures 7.5 (10: 15: 20: 22.5)cm/3 (4: 6: 8: 9)in from cast-on edge, ending with a WS row.

Next row (RS) K22 (26: 31: 43: 48); work next 14 sts in cable panel patt as set; k22 (26: 31: 43: 48).

Next row P22 (26: 31: 43: 48); work next 14 sts in cable panel patt as set; p22 (26: 31: 43: 48).

This sets patt with st st at each side of central 14-st cable panel.

Cont in patt as now set until cable panel measures 14 (17.5: 28: 33: 35.5)cm/ 5¹/₂ (7: 11: 13: 14)in from cast-on edge, ending with a WS row.

(**Note:** If required, increase or reduce length of coat here and match this change on gusset.)

Mark for leg openings
Mark each end of last row with a coloured thread to indicate beg of leg openings.
Cont in patt until cable panel measures 20 (25.5: 35.5: 40.5: 44.5)cm/ 8 (10: 14: 16: 17¹/₂)in from cast-on edge, ending with a WS row.
Mark each end of last row with a coloured thread to indicate end of leg openings.
Cont in patt until cable panel measures 25.5 (30.5: 40.5: 45.5: 50.5)cm/ 10 (12: 16: 18: 20)in from cast-on edge, ending with a WS row.

Next row (RS) K8 (10: 12: 18: 20), k2tog, k12 (14: 17: 23: 26); work next 14 sts in cable panel patt as set; k12 (14: 17: 23: 26), k2tog, k8 (10: 12: 18: 20). (56 (64: 74: 98: 108) sts.)

Next row P21 (25: 30: 42: 47); work next 14 sts in cable panel patt as set; p21 (25: 30: 42: 47).

Next row K8 (10: 12: 18: 20), k2tog, k11 (13: 16: 22: 25); work next 14 sts in cable panel patt as set; k11 (13: 16: 22: 25), k2tog, k8 (10: 12: 18: 20). (54 (62: 72: 96: 106) sts.)

Working in patt as set, cont to dec 1 st at each end of 4 (6: 7: 13: 13) foll alt rows (RS rows), ending with a RS row. (46 (50: 58: 70: 80) sts.)

Work straight in patt until cable panel measures 30.5 (35.5: 45.5: 55.5: 61)cm/12 (14: 18: 22: 24)in from cast-on edge, ending with a WS row.

Break off yarn and leave sts on a st holder.

GUSSET

With 3.25mm (US size 3) needles, cast on 16 (22: 28: 34: 38) sts.
Work 6 rows in k1, p1 rib as for top of coat.
Change to 4mm (US size 6) needles.
Beg with a k row, work in st st until gusset measures 6.5 (7.5: 13: 13: 13)cm/ 3¹/₂ (3: 5: 5: 5)in from cast-on edge, ending with a p row.

Mark for leg openings
Mark each end of last row with a coloured thread to indicate beg of leg openings.
Cont in st st throughout, work until leg openings measure same as leg openings on top of coat, ending with a p row.
Mark each end of last row with a coloured thread to indicate end of leg openings.
Work until gusset measures 20 (21.5: 26.5: 25.5: 30.5)cm/8 (8¹/₂: 10¹/₂: 10: 12)in from cast-on edge, ending with a p row.

Dec 1 st at each end of next 4 (6: 9: 11: 12) rows, ending with a p (p: k: k: p) row. (8 (10: 10: 12: 14) sts.)

Work straight until gusset measures 23 (25.5: 30.5: 35.5: 38.5)cm/ 9 (10: 12: 14: 15)in from cast-on edge, ending with a p row.

Do not break off yarn and leave sts on a st holder.

TO FINISH

Press top of coat and gusset lightly on wrong side, following instructions on yarn label and avoiding cable panel.

With right sides together and matching leg-opening markers, sew right side edge of top of coat to left side edge of gusset, leaving seam open between markers for front-leg openings.

Polo-neck collar
With RS facing and 3.25mm (US size 3) needles, k 8 (10: 10: 12: 14) sts from gusset st holder and k 46 (50: 58: 70: 80) sts from top-of-coat st holder. (54 (60: 68: 82: 94) sts.)

Work these sts in k1, p1 rib until collar measures 10 (10: 12.5: 15: 15)cm/ 4 (4: 5: 6: 6)in.

Cast off loosely in rib.

With right sides together, sew remaining side seam as for first side seam, and sew collar seam reversing seam on last 5 (5: 6.5: 7.5: 7.5)cm/2 (2: 2¹/₂: 3: 3)in of collar for turnback.

SPOT **DOG** COAT

LEVEL
Intermediate

SIZES
See page 10 for dog measurements and sizes.

FINISHED COAT MEASUREMENTS

	Width of coat	Length to neck shaping
Extra small	25cm/10in	25cm/10in
Small	35.5cm/14in	33cm/13in
Medium	39cm/15^1/2in	40.5cm/16in
Large	43cm/17in	50.5cm/20in
Extra large	50cm/19^3/4in	56cm/22in

MATERIALS
2 (2: 2: 3: 4) x 50g/1^3/4oz balls of Jaeger *Matchmaker Merino DK* in main colour **MC**, for background
Small amount of Jaeger *Matchmaker Merino DK* in each of 6 different colours, for spot motifs
Pair of 3.25mm (US size 3) knitting needles
Pair of 4mm (US size 6) knitting needles
4 (5: 5: 5: 5) buttons

TENSION
22 sts and 30 rows to 10cm/4in measured over st st using 4mm (US size 6) needles.

ABBREVIATIONS
See page 17.

CHART NOTE
The chart is worked in st st. When working from the chart, read odd-numbered rows (k rows) from right to left, and even-numbered rows (p rows) from left to right. When working the chart pattern, use the intarsia method (see page 14), knitting with a separate small ball (or long length) of yarn for each area of colour and twisting yarns together on wrong side when changing colour to avoid holes.
Note: The chart shows only the st st section of the coat; the moss stitch borders are not included on the chart.

TO MAKE COAT
With 3.25mm (US size 3) needles and MC, cast on 42 (64: 72: 80: 96) sts.
Work border in moss st as follows:
1st row (RS) *K1, p1; rep from * to end.
2nd row P1, k1; rep from * to end.
3rd row [K1, p1] twice, k into front and back of next st, *p1, k1; rep from * to last 7 sts, p1, k into front and back of next st, [p1, k1] twice, p1.
(44 (66: 74: 82: 98) sts.)
4th row [P1, k1] 3 times, k next st (inc st), p1, k1; rep from * to last 7 sts, p1, k next st (inc st), [k1, p1] twice, k1.
5th row [K1, p1] twice, k into front and

back of next st, *k1, p1; rep from * to last 7 sts, k into front and back of next st, [k1, p1] 3 times.
(46 (68: 76: 84: 100) sts.)
6th row Rep 2nd row.
Change to 4mm (US size 6) needles.
Cont to shape coat, beg st st patt with moss st side borders as follows:
1st patt row (RS) K1, [p1, k1] twice for moss st border; k into front and back of next st, k to last 6 sts, k into front and back of next st; p1, [k1, p1] twice for moss st border.
2nd patt row P1, [k1, p1] twice for moss st border; p to last 5 sts; k1, [p1, k1]

twice for moss st border.

3rd and 4th patt rows Rep 1st and 2nd patt rows. (*50 (72: 80: 88: 104) sts.*)
Set position of chart patt (see page 127) on next 2 rows (chart rows 5 and 6) as follows:

5th patt row (RS) Using MC moss st 5 sts; using MC k into front and back of next st, k0 (2: 6: 1: 0)MC, [k2 in chosen spot colour, k16MC] 2 (3: 3: 4: 5) times, k2 in chosen spot colour, k0 (2: 6: 1: 0)MC, using MC k into front and back of next st; using MC moss st 5 sts.
(*52 (74: 82: 90: 106) sts.*)

6th patt row Using MC moss st 5 sts; p1 (3: 7: 2: 1)MC, [p4 in random spot colour, p14MC] 2 (3: 3: 4: 5) times, p4 in random spot colour, using MC p to last 5 sts; moss st 5 sts.
Cont foll chart as set and working 5-st moss st borders **and at the same time** cont to inc 1 st at each end (inside moss st borders) of 2 foll alt rows (RS rows), ending with a RS row.
(*56 (78: 86: 94: 110) sts.*)
Work straight in patt as set, using colours at random for spots, until chart row 36 has been completed, ending with a WS row.
Cont straight in patt, repeating chart rows 13–36 for spot patt, until coat measures 25 (33: 40.5: 50.5: 56)cm/10 (13: 16: 20: 22)in from cast-on edge, ending with a WS row in MC only.
(**Note:** If you need to lengthen coat to fit your dog, work some extra rows here before starting neck shaping.)

Shape neck

Next row (RS) Work 23 (34: 36: 38: 44) sts in patt, then turn, leaving rem sts on a st holder.
Working on these sts only, cont as follows:
**Keeping patt correct throughout, dec 1 st at neck edge of next 3 rows.
Dec 1 st at neck edge of 4 (4: 4: 2: 4) foll alt rows.
Dec 1 st at neck edge of every 4th row 1 (1: 1: 2: 1) times.
(*15 (26: 28: 31: 36) sts.*)
Work straight until coat measures 33 (43: 53: 66: 73.5)cm/13 (17: 21: 26: 29)in from cast-on edge, ending with a WS row.
Change to 3.25mm (US size 3) needles and MC only.**
Work 2 rows in moss st, ending with a WS row.

Small, Medium, Large and Extra Large only
Next row (buttonhole row) (RS) Moss st – (3: 5: 8: 13) sts, [work 2tog, yon, moss st 7 sts] twice, work 2tog, yon, moss st 3 sts.

Extra Small only
Next row (buttonhole row) (RS) Moss st 1 st, work 2tog, yon, moss st 7 sts, work 2tog, yon, moss st 3 sts.

All sizes
Work 3 rows in moss st.
Cast off.
With RS facing, return to rem sts, slip centre 10 (10: 14: 18: 22) sts onto a st holder, rejoin yarn and work in patt to end.
Work as for first side of neck from ** to **.
Work 6 rows in moss st.
Cast off.

STRAP

With 3.25mm (US size 3) needles and MC, cast on 13 sts.
1st row *K1, p1; rep from * to last st, k1.
(Last row is repeated to form moss st.)
Work in moss st until strap measures 5 (11: 15: 24: 28)cm/2 (4½: 6: 9½: 11)in from cast-on edge.
Next row (buttonhole row) Moss st 5 sts, work 2tog, yon, moss st 6 sts.
Work in moss st until strap measures 7.5 (14: 17.5: 26.5: 30.5)cm/3 (5½: 7: 10½: 12)in from cast-on edge.
Rep buttonhole row.
Work in moss st until strap measures 10 (16.5: 20.5: 29: 33)cm/4 (6½: 8: 11½: 13)in from cast-on edge.
Rep buttonhole row.

Work in moss st until strap measures 12.5 (19: 22.5: 30.5: 35.5) cm/5 (7½: 9: 12: 14) in from cast-on edge.
Cast off.

TO FINISH

Block and press coat lightly on wrong side, following instructions on yarn label and avoiding moss st borders. Do not press strap.

Neck edging
With RS facing, 3.25mm needles (US size 3) and MC, pick up and knit 22 (28: 32: 36: 40) sts along right neck edge (picking up first 5 sts along edge of moss st border), knit 10 (10: 14: 18: 22) sts from centre neck st holder, pick up and knit 22 (28: 32: 36: 40) sts up left neck edge.
(*54 (66: 78: 90: 102) sts.*)
Work 2 rows in moss st, ending with a RS row.
Next row (buttonhole row) (WS) Moss st to last 4 sts, yon, work 2tog, moss st 2 sts (buttonhole should be in line with other buttonholes).
Work 2 rows more in moss st.
Cast off.
Sew 3 (4: 4: 4: 4) buttons to front opening border to correspond with buttonholes.
Sew strap to right side-edge of coat 14 (20.5: 26.5: 33.5: 38)cm/5½ (8: 10½: 13: 15)in from cast-on edge.
Sew button for strap to wrong side of left side-edge of coat to correspond with position of strap.

FLORAL **DOG** COAT

LEVEL
Difficult

SIZES
See page 10 for dog measurements and sizes.

FINISHED COAT MEASUREMENTS

	Width of coat	Length to neck shaping
Extra small	25.5cm/10in	25cm/10in
Small	35.5cm/14in	33cm/13in
Medium	39cm/15½in	40.5cm/16in
Large	43cm/17in	50.5cm/20in
Extra large	50cm/19¾in	56cm/22in

MATERIALS
2 (2: 2: 3: 4) x 50g/1¾oz balls of Jaeger *Matchmaker Merino DK* in main colour **MC**, for background
1 x 50g/1¾oz ball of Jaeger *Matchmaker Merino DK* in each of 4 different colours – **A**, **B**, **C** and **D** – for motifs
Pair of 3.25mm (US size 3) knitting needles
Pair of 4mm (US size 6) knitting needles
4 (5: 5: 5: 5) buttons

TENSION
22 sts and 30 rows to 10cm/4in measured over st st using 4mm (US size 6) needles.

ABBREVIATIONS
See page 17.

CHART NOTE
The chart is worked in st st. When working from the chart, read odd-numbered rows (k rows) from right to left, and even-numbered rows (p rows) from left to right.
When working the chart pattern, use the intarsia method (see page 14), knitting with a separate small ball (or long length) of yarn for each area of colour and twisting yarns together on wrong side when changing colour to avoid holes.
Note: The chart shows only the st st section of the coat; the moss stitch borders are not included on the chart.

TO MAKE COAT
With 3.25mm (US size 3) needles and MC, cast on 42 (64: 72: 80: 96) sts.
Work border in moss st as follows:
1st row (RS) *K1, p1; rep from * to end.
2nd row P1, k1; rep from * to end.
3rd row [K1, p1] twice, k into front and back of next st, *p1, k1; rep from * to last 7 sts, p1, k into front and back of next st, [p1, k1] twice, p1.
(44 (66: 74: 82: 98) sts.)
4th row [P1, k1] 3 times, k next st (the inc st), p1, k1; rep from * to last 7 sts, p1, k next st (the inc st), [k1, p1] twice, k1.

5th row [K1, p1] twice, k into front and back of next st, *k1, p1; rep from * to last 7 sts, k into front and back of next st, [k1, p1] 3 times.
(46 (68: 76: 84: 100) sts.)
6th row Rep 2nd row.
Change to 4mm (US size 6) needles.
Cont to shape coat, beg st st patt with moss st side borders as follows:
1st patt row (RS) K1, [k1, k1] twice for moss st border; k into front and back of next st, k to last 6 sts, k into front and back of next st; p1, [k1, p1] twice for moss st border.

41

2nd patt row P1, [k1, p1] twice for moss st border; p to last 5 sts; k1, [p1, k1] twice for moss st border.

3rd and 4th patt rows Rep 1st and 2nd patt rows. *(50 (72: 80: 88: 104) sts.)*
Set position of chart patt (see pages 128–129) on next 2 rows (chart rows 5 and 6) as follows:

5th patt row (RS) Using MC moss st 5 sts; using MC k into front and back of next st, k27 (38: 42: 46: 54)MC, k4A, k7 (18: 22: 26: 34)MC, using MC k into front and back of next st; using MC moss st 5 sts. *(52 (74: 82: 90: 106) sts.)*

6th patt row Using MC moss st 5 sts; p3 (14: 18: 22: 30)MC, p3A, p2MC, p6A, using MC p to last 5 sts; moss st 5 sts.
Cont foll chart as set and working 5-st moss st borders **and at the same time** cont to inc 1 st at each end (inside moss st borders) of 2 foll alt rows (RS rows), ending with a RS row.
(56 (78: 86: 94: 110) sts.)
Work straight in patt as set (when chart patt has been completed, cont using MC only) until coat measures 25 (33: 40.5: 50.5: 56)cm/10 (13: 16: 20: 22)in from cast-on edge, ending with a WS row.
(**Note:** If you need to lengthen coat to fit your dog, work some extra rows here before starting neck shaping.)

Shape neck
Next row (RS) Work 23 (34: 36: 38: 44) sts in patt, then turn, leaving rem sts on a st holder.
Working on these sts only, cont as follows:
**Keeping patt correct throughout, dec 1 st at neck edge of next 3 rows.
Dec 1 st at neck edge of 4 (4: 4: 2: 4) foll alt rows.
Dec 1 st at neck edge of every 4th row 1 (1: 1: 2: 1) times. *(15 (26: 28: 31: 36) sts.)*

Work straight until coat measures 33 (43: 53: 66: 73.5)cm/13 (17: 21: 26: 29)in from cast-on edge, ending with a WS row. Change to 3.25mm (US size 3) needles and MC only.**
Work 2 rows in moss st, ending with a WS row.

Small, Medium, Large and Extra Large only
Next row (buttonhole row) (RS) Moss st – (3: 5: 8: 13) sts, [work 2tog, yon, moss st 7 sts] twice, work 2tog, yon, moss st 3 sts.

Extra Small only
Next row (buttonhole row) (RS) Moss st 1 st, work 2tog, yon, moss st 7 sts, work 2tog, yon, moss st 3 sts.

All sizes
Work 3 rows in moss st.
Cast off.
With RS facing, return to rem sts, slip centre 10 (10: 14: 18: 22) sts onto a st holder, rejoin yarn and work in patt to end.
Work as for first side of neck from ** to **.
Work 6 rows in moss st.
Cast off.

STRAP
With 3.25mm (US size 3) needles and MC, cast on 13 sts.
1st row *K1, p1; rep from * to last st, k1. (Last row is repeated to form moss st.)
Work in moss st until strap measures 5 (11: 15: 24: 28)cm/2 (4½: 6: 9½: 11)in from cast-on edge.
Next row (buttonhole row) Moss st 5 sts, work 2tog, yon, moss st 6 sts.
Work in moss st until strap measures 7.5 (14: 17.5: 26.5: 30.5)cm/3 (5½: 7: 10½: 12)in from cast-on edge.

Rep buttonhole row.
Work in moss st until strap measures 10 (16.5: 20.5: 29: 33)cm/4 (6½: 8: 11½: 13)in from cast-on edge.
Rep buttonhole row.
Work in moss st until strap measures 12.5 (19: 22.5: 30.5: 35.5) cm/ 5 (7½: 9: 12: 14) in from cast-on edge.
Cast off.

TO FINISH
Block and press coat lightly on wrong side, following instructions on yarn label and avoiding moss st borders. Do not press strap.

Neck edging
With RS facing, 3.25mm (US size 3) needles and MC, pick up and knit 22 (28: 32: 36: 40) sts along right neck edge (picking up first 5 sts along edge of moss st border), knit 10 (10: 14: 18: 22) sts from centre neck st holder, pick up and knit 22 (28: 32: 36: 40) sts up left neck edge. *(54 (66: 78: 90: 102) sts.)*
Work 2 rows in moss st, ending with a RS row.
Next row (buttonhole row) (WS) Moss st to last 4 sts, yon, work 2tog, moss st 2 sts (buttonhole should be in line with other buttonholes).
Work 2 rows more in moss st.
Cast off.
Sew 3 (4: 4: 4: 4) buttons to front opening border to correspond with buttonholes.
Sew strap to right side-edge of coat 14 (20.5: 26.5: 33:5: 38)cm/5½ (8: 10½: 13: 15)in from cast-on edge. Sew button for strap to wrong side of left side-edge of coat to correspond with position of strap.

CAT CUSHIONS

Here are three designs for you to make for your beloved cat. The plain one is extremely simple, but has tassels on the corners for your cat to toy with during those moments of ennui; the baroque is grander in style; and the heraldic is appropriately aristocratic for the most princely of pets.

TASSELS **CAT** CUSHION

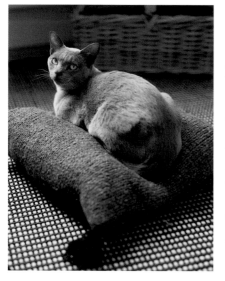

LEVEL
Easy ◀‹‹‹‹‹‹◀

SIZE
The finished cushion measures approximately 46cm/18in square.

MATERIALS
3 x 100g/3¹/₂oz balls of Rowan *Scottish Tweed Chunky* in main colour **MC**, for cushion
Small amount of a double-knitting-weight yarn in a contrasting colour **A**, for tassels
Pair of 8mm (US size 11) knitting needles
Cushion pad to fit

TENSION
12 sts and 16 rows to 10cm/4in measured over st st using 8mm (US size 11) needles.

ABBREVIATIONS
See page 17.

TO MAKE CUSHION COVER
With 8mm (US size 11) needles, cast on 54 sts.
Beg with a k row, work in st st until cushion measures 92cm/36in from cast-on edge, ending with a p row.
Cast off.

TO FINISH
Press lightly on wrong side, following instructions on yarn label.
Sew cast-on edge of knitting to cast-off edge.

With cover right-side out, position seam just worked in centre back of cushion; then sew one side seam using mattress stitch. Insert cushion pad and sew other side seam in same way.

Tassels (make 4)
Cut a piece of cardboard 5cm/2in wide by 10cm/4in long. Wind A around length of card 25 times. Then thread a needle with a length of A and pass it under wrapped yarn at one end of cardboard.

Tie yarn tightly, leaving two long tail ends. Cut through strands of yarn at other end of cardboard. Wind one long tail end of yarn tightly around tassel approximately 2cm/³/₄in from uncut end and secure. Use remaining length of yarn to sew tassel to one corner of cushion.
Make three more tassels in same way and sew one to each of the three remaining corners.

BAROQUE **CAT** CUSHION

LEVEL
Intermediate ◄≪≪≪◄ ◄≪≪≪◄

SIZE
The finished cushion measures approximately 45.5cm/18in square.

MATERIALS
3 x 50g/1$\frac{3}{4}$oz balls of Rowan *Pure Wool DK* in main colour **MC**
1 x 50g/1$\frac{3}{4}$oz ball of Rowan *Pure Wool DK* in a contrasting colour **A**
Pair of 4mm (US size 6) knitting needles
Cushion pad to fit

TENSION
22 sts and 30 rows to 10cm/4in over st st using 4mm (US size 6) needles.

ABBREVIATIONS
See page 17.

CHART NOTE
The chart is worked in st st. When working from the chart, read odd-numbered rows (k rows) from right to left, and even-numbered rows (p rows) from left to right. When working the chart pattern, use the intarsia method (see page 14), knitting with a separate small ball (or long length) of yarn for each area of colour and twisting yarns together on wrong side when changing colour to avoid holes.

CUSHION COVER FRONT
With 4mm (US size 6) needles and MC, cast on 100 sts.
Beg with a k row, work 4 rows in st st, ending with a p row.
Set position of chart patt (see page 130) on next 2 rows (chart rows 5 and 6) as follows:
Next row (RS) Using MC k35, using A k8, using MC k14, using A k8, using MC k35.
Next row Using MC p34, using A p11, using MC k10, using A p11, using MC p34.
Cont in st st following chart until chart row 132 has been completed, ending with a p row.
Using MC only and beg with a k row, work 4 rows in st st.
Cast off.

CUSHION COVER BACK
With 4mm (US size 6) needles and MC, cast on 100 sts.
Beg with a k row, work 136 rows in st st.
Cast off.

TO FINISH
Block and press both pieces lightly on wrong side, following instructions on yarn label.
With right sides together, sew front to back leaving one side open.
Turn cover right side out.
Insert cushion pad and sew remaining seam.

HERALDIC **CAT** CUSHION

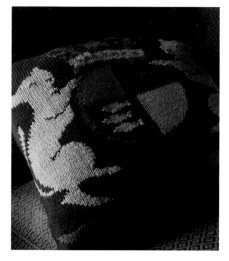

LEVEL
Intermediate ◀≪≪≪◀ ◀≪≪≪◀

SIZE
The finished cushion measures approximately 45.5cm/18in square.

MATERIALS
2 x 50g/1¾oz balls of Jaeger *Matchmaker Merino DK* in main colour **MC** (black/Black 681), for background
1 x 50g/1¾oz ball of Jaeger *Matchmaker Merino DK* in each of **A** (violet/Geranium 894), **B** (ochre/Syrup 789) and **C** (teal/Teal 790), for motifs
Pair of 4mm (US size 6) knitting needles
Cushion pad to fit

TENSION
22 sts and 30 rows to 10cm/4in measured over st st using 4mm (US size 6) needles.

ABBREVIATIONS
See page 17.

YARN NOTE
The colours listed in the Materials list are there merely as a suggestion. Feel free to pick your own selection of four different colours to customize the cushion. You can use Jaeger *Matchmaker Merino DK*, Rowan *Pure Wool DK*, or any other yarn of the same weight.

CHART NOTE
The chart is worked in st st. When working from the chart, read odd-numbered rows (k rows) from right to left, and even-numbered rows (p rows) from left to right. When working the chart pattern, use the intarsia method (see page 14), knitting with a separate small ball (or long length) of yarn for each area of colour and twisting yarns together on wrong side when changing colour to avoid holes.

CUSHION COVER FRONT
With 4mm (US size 6) needles and MC, cast on 100 sts.
Beg with a k row, work 4 rows in st st, ending with a p row.
Set position of chart patt (see page 131) on next 2 rows (chart rows 5 and 6) as follows:
Next row (RS) Using MC k46, using A k8, using MC k46.
Next row Using MC p44, using A p12, using MC p44.
Cont in st st following chart until chart row 132 has been completed, ending with a p row.
Using MC only and beg with a k row, work 4 rows in st st.
Cast off.

CUSHION COVER BACK
With 4mm (US size 6) needles and MC, cast on 100 sts.
Beg with a k row, work 136 rows in st st.
Cast off.

TO FINISH
Block and press both pieces lightly on wrong side, following instructions on yarn label.
With right sides together, sew front to back leaving one side open.
Turn cover right side out.
Insert cushion pad and sew remaining seam.

WATER LILY

Don't neglect your goldfish. Here is your chance to knit this beautiful water lily for no cost. In an evening, using carrier bags from high street shops, you can decorate your fish tank. Try making several lilies and float them in your pond outside. So much easier to look after than the real thing.

WATER LILY

LEVEL
Easy

SIZE
The finished water lily measures approximately 10–12cm/4–4³⁄₄in in diameter and each leaf measures approximately 9–10cm/3¹⁄₂–4in in length.

MATERIALS
One green plastic bag, to make 'yarn' **A** for leaves
One white or pink plastic bag, to make 'yarn' **B** for petals
One orange plastic bag, to make 'yarn' **C** for stamens
Pair of 4mm (US size 6) knitting needles
Matching sewing thread, for sewing together petals and sewing on stamens

TENSION
It is not necessary to knit to a specific tension to make the water lily. The size will vary (see Size above) according to the thickness of the plastic used for the 'yarn', the width of the plastic strips and the knitter's individual tension.

ABBREVIATIONS
See page 17.

SPECIAL NOTE
The plastic 'yarn' is knitted in garter stitch in the usual way. The 'yarn' will stretch while you are knitting with it, so be careful not to pull it too tightly because this might break it, and the more breaks the more knots and the more tails ends you will have to darn in later.

TO PREPARE PLASTIC 'YARN'
Using scissors, cut off the bottom and handles of each bag (including gusset), so that it forms a large tube.
Cut each bag into a continuous 'yarn' strip as follows:
Open out bag. Then starting at the bottom of bag, cut a continuous strip of plastic in a spiral (as you would peel an apple), about 1cm/³⁄₈in wide. If the bag has printing on it, you can either cut out that section or incorporate into your knitting 'yarn'. Loosely wind the strip into a ball as you proceed.

If the plastic breaks while you are preparing it, just knot the strips together.

LEAVES (MAKE 2)
With 4mm (US size 6) needles and A, cast on 4 sts.
Knit 1 row.
Cont in garter st throughout, inc 1 st at each end of next row 5 rows. (*14 sts.*)
Knit 1 row.
Inc 1 st at each end of next row. (*16 sts.*)
Work straight in garter st for 10 rows.

Divide leaf
Before beg next row to divide leaf, mark this side of work as RS, using a coloured thread.
Next row (RS) K8, then turn, leaving rem sts on a st holder.
Working on these 8 sts only, cont as follows:
Knit 1 row.
Dec 1 st at beg of next row (outer leaf edge). (*7 sts.*)

Knit 1 row.
Dec 1 st at beg of next row. (*6 sts.*)
Dec 1 st at outer leaf edge on each of next 4 rows. (*2 sts.*)
Cast off.
With RS facing, rejoin A to 8 sts on holder leaving a tail end 20cm/8in long (for attaching leaves to flowers), then k to end.
Knit 1 row.
Dec 1 st at end of next row (outer leaf edge). (*7 sts.*)
Knit 1 row.
Dec 1 st at end of next row. (*6 sts.*)
Dec 1 st at outer leaf edge on each of next 4 rows. (*2 sts.*)
Cast off.
Make 1 more leaf in same way.

SMALL INNER PETALS (MAKE 5)
With 4mm (US size 6) needles and B, cast on 5 sts.
Knit 1 row.
Cont in garter st throughout, inc 1 st at

each end of next row. (*7 sts.*)
Work straight in garter st for 8 rows.
Dec 1 st at each end of next 2 rows. (*3 sts.*)
Next row K2tog, k1.
Next row K2tog, then break off B, thread
tail end through rem st and pull to fasten off.
Make 4 more inner petals in same way.

LARGE OUTER PETALS (MAKE 5)
With 4mm (US size 6) needles and B,
cast on 7 sts.
Knit 1 row.
Cont in garter st throughout, inc 1 st at
each end of next row. (*9 sts.*)
Knit 1 row.
Inc 1 st at each end of next row. (*11 sts.*)
Work straight in garter st for 8 rows.
Dec 1 st at each end of next 4 rows. (*3 sts.*)
Next row K2tog, k1.
Next row K2tog, then break off B, thread

tail end through rem st and pull to fasten off.
Make 4 more outer petals in same way,
leaving a 20cm/8in tail end on 2 of them
when casting on, to attach flowers to leaves.

STAMENS (MAKE 3)
With 4mm (US size 6) needles and C,
cast on 8 sts.
Cast off.
Make 2 more stamens in same way.

TO FINISH
Darn in ends of plastic 'yarn', but leave ends
left long on purpose (on leaves and two of
large outer petals).
Take two large petals and overlap them so
that one is on top of half of the other, with
cast-on edges aligned. Using a sewing
needle and matching thread, sew these
two petals together along cast-on edge,

slightly gathering base of petals. Continue
sewing on remaining three large petals to
first two in same way, overlapping each
added petal and slightly gathering along
base to form a ring of petals. (Leave two
long tail ends at back of flower.) Sew
together five small petals in same way to
make a ring, then sew to centre of ring of
large petals. Sew three stamens to centre
of water lily, using matching sewing thread.
Secure thread to back of flower. Pull petals
upward to make water lily look realistic.
Underneath flower, knot together two long
tail ends from flower and two from leaves,
about 2.5cm/1in away from flowers and
leaves. Then to form a trailing 'root', plait
together these tail ends (using two flower
tail ends as one strand) and knot together
at end. Trim ends close to knot.

HORSE BLANKET

From trekking in the Camargue to the Cheltenham
Gold Cup, your horse will delight in this luxurious
blanket. Make him the envy of his stablemates
by customising it. Add more squares, his name,
the date he won the Derby (or not) or his colours,
for a unique equine heirloom.

HORSE BLANKET

LEVEL
Intermediate

SIZE
The finished horse blanket measures approximately 80cm/31¹/₂in wide by 100cm/39¹/₂in long. (Each individual square measures 20cm/8in.)
Note: If you would like to increase the size of the blanket, add more squares.

MATERIALS
1 x 50g/1³/₄oz ball of Jaeger *Matchmaker Merino DK* in each of 9 different colours:
A (charcoal/Charcoal 783), **B** (dark brown/Bison 728), **C** (mid blue/Mariner 629), **D** (violet/Geranium 894), **E** (camel/Syrup 789), **F** (lilac/Dusk 626), **H** (purple/Buddleia 856), **L** (black/Black 728) and **M** (teal/Teal 790)
2 x 50g/1³/₄oz balls of Jaeger *Matchmaker Merino DK* in each of 3 different colours:
G (red/Clarice 876), **J** (light green/Sage 857) and **K** (light blue/Marine 914)
Pair of 4mm (US 6) knitting needles

TENSION
22 sts and 30 rows to 10cm/4in measured over st st using 4mm (US size 6) needles.

ABBREVIATIONS
See page 17.

YARN NOTE
The colours listed in the Materials list are there merely to give you an idea for a colour combination. Feel free to pick your own selection of 12 different colours to customize the blanket to make it your own. You can use Jaeger *Matchmaker Merino DK*, Rowan *Pure Wool DK*, or any other yarn of the same weight.

CHART NOTE
The charts are worked in st st. When working from the charts, read odd-numbered rows (k rows) from right to left, and even-numbered rows (p rows) from left to right.
When working the chart patterns, use the intarsia method (see page 14), knitting

with a separate small ball (or long length) of yarn for each area of colour and twisting yarns together on wrong side when changing colour to avoid holes.

SQUARE 1 – BRIDLE BITS
With 4mm (US size 6) needles and M, cast on 44 sts.
Beg with a k row and chart row 1, work in st st following bridle bits chart (see page 132) until all 60 chart rows have been completed. Cast off.

SQUARE 2 – PLAIN
With 4mm (US size 6) needles and J, cast on 44 sts.
Beg with a k row, work 60 rows in st st. Cast off.

SQUARE 3 – RODEO
With 4mm (US size 6) needles and D, cast on 44 sts.
Beg with a k row and chart row 1, work in st st following rodeo chart (see page 132) until all 60 chart rows have been completed. Cast off.

SQUARE 4 – NARROW STRIPES
With 4mm (US size 6) needles and E, cast on 44 sts.
Beg with a k row, work in st st in stripes as follows:
4 rows E, 4 rows G, 4 rows J, 4 rows F.
Rep from * to * twice more.
Cont in st st, work 4 rows E, 4 rows G and 4 rows J – a total of 60 rows worked

from cast-on edge.
Cast off.

SQUARE 5 – BROAD STRIPES
With 4mm (US size 6) needles and J,
cast on 44 sts.
Beg with a k row, work in st st in stripes
as follows:
6 rows J, 6 rows F, 6 rows K.
Rep from ** to ** twice more.
Cont in st st, work 6 rows J – a total of
60 rows worked from cast-on edge.
Cast off.

SQUARE 6 – SMALL CHECKS
With 4mm (US size 6) needles and A,
cast on 44 sts (if desired, cast on with
colours to match first chart row).
Beg with a k row and chart row 1, work
in st st following small checks chart (see
page 133) until all 60 chart rows have
been completed. Cast off.

SQUARE 7 – PLAIN
Work as for square 2, but using K.

SQUARE 8 – ROSETTE
With 4mm (US size 6) needles and J,
cast on 44 sts.
Beg with a k row and chart row 1,
work in st st following rosette chart (see
page 133) until all 60 chart rows have
been completed. Cast off.

SQUARE 9 – HORSESHOE
With 4mm (US size 6) needles and K,
cast on 44 sts.
Beg with a k row and chart row 1, work
in st st following horseshoe chart (see page
134) until all 60 chart rows have been
completed. Cast off.

SQUARE 10 – PLAIN
Work as for square 2, but using M.

SQUARE 11 – BRIDLE BITS
Work as for square 1, but using B for
background instead of M.

SQUARE 12 – PLAIN
Work as for square 2, but using C.

SQUARE 13 – PLAIN
Work as for square 2, but using B.

SQUARE 14 – BIG CHECKS
With 4mm (US size 6) needles and K, cast
on 44 sts (if desired, cast on with colours
to match first chart row).
Beg with a k row and chart row 1, work
in st st following big checks chart (see
page 134) until all 60 chart rows have
been completed. Cast off.

SQUARE 15 – NAME
With 4mm (US size 6) needles and J,
cast on 44 sts.
Beg with a k row and chart row 1,
work in st st following name chart (see
Note below) until all 60 chart rows have
been completed.
Cast off.
(Note: Use chart on page 135, or if
desired, insert your own horse's name,
using alphabet chart on page 140.)

SQUARE 16 – RODEO
Work as for square 3, but using F for
background instead of D.

SQUARE 17 – SPOTS
With 4mm (US size 6) needles and H,
cast on 44 sts.
Beg with a k row and chart row 1,
work in st st following spots chart (see
page 135) until all 60 chart rows have
been completed. Cast off.

SQUARE 18 – PLAIN
Work as for square 2, but using F.

SQUARE 19 – SPOTS
Work as for square 17, but using D for
background and M for spots.

SQUARE 20 – PLAIN
Work as for square 2, but using G.

TO FINISH
Block and press all 20 squares lightly
on wrong side, following instructions on
yarn label.

Lay out squares on floor to make a
patchwork four squares wide by five
squares long. Make your own arrangement
to customise your blanket; or arrange as
for blanket pictured – using squares 1–4
(from left to right) for the top row, squares
5–8 (from left to right) for the second row
down, and so on. (Note: Position the
rodeo and rosette in top half of blanket
upside down so that when blanket is on
horse, they will be upright.)
To sew squares together, take the first two
squares from a vertical row of squares and
with right sides together, sew them together
along cast-on/cast-off edges, using
overcast stitch and a yarn that matches
one of the squares.
Sew together all five squares in the first
vertical row.
Then sew together remaining vertical rows
(of five squares each) in same way.
Pin and sew all these four strips together.
Press again.

MOUSE MAT FOR CAT

An absolutely vital lounging accessory for cats.
Quick to knit, yet stylish to have about the house,
it implies tremendous bravery with the giant mouse
skin whilst also keeping cat hairs off the furniture.

MOUSE MAT FOR CAT

LEVEL
Easy

SIZE
The finished mouse mat measures approximately 40cm/15¾in wide across the body and 75cm/29½in long from nose to tail.
Note: If your cat is enormous, you can make the mat bigger by adding more stitches and rows in the centre.

MATERIALS
2 x 100g/3½oz balls of Rowan *Scottish Tweed Chunky* in main colour **MC**, for mat and back of ears
Small amount of Rowan *Scottish Tweed Chunky* in a contrasting colour **A**, for inside of ears, nose and whiskers
Small amount of double-knitting-weight yarn that matches MC, for sewing ear fronts to backs
Pair of 8mm (US size 11) knitting needles
2 black buttons, for eyes
Crochet hook, for attaching whiskers

TENSION
11 sts and 19 rows to 10cm/4in measured over garter st using 8mm (US size 11) needles.

ABBREVIATIONS
See page 17.

TO MAKE MOUSE MAT
The whole body and tail of mouse mat is knitted in garter st, starting at tail end.

Shape tail
With 8mm (US size 11) needles and MC, cast on 2 sts.
Work 12 rows in garter st (knit every row).
Cont in garter st throughout, inc 1 st at each end of next row. (4 sts.)
Work straight for 11 rows.
Inc 1 st at each end of next row. (6 sts.)
Work straight for 11 rows.

Begin body
Cast on 12 sts at end of next 2 rows. (30 sts.)
Work straight for 1 row.

Inc 1 st at each end of next 9 rows. (48 sts.)
Work straight for 2 rows.

Shape back legs
**Cast on 10 sts at end of next 2 rows. (68 sts.)
Inc 1 st at each end of next 3 rows. (74 sts.)
Work straight for 4 rows.
Dec 1 st at each end of next 3 rows. (68 sts.)
Cast off 12 sts at beg of next 2 rows. (44 sts.)**
Work straight for 36 rows.

Shape front legs
Rep from ** to ** once more.

Work straight for 1 row.

Shape neck and head
Cast off 5 sts at beg of next 2 rows. (34 sts.)
Cast off 4 sts at beg of next 2 rows. (26 sts.)
Cast off 2 sts at beg of next 2 rows. (22 sts.)
Work straight for 4 rows.
Dec 1 st at each end of next row and then at each end of 2 foll 4th rows. (16 sts.)
Dec 1 st at each end of 3 foll alt rows. (10 sts.)
Dec 1 st at each end of next 4 rows. (2 sts.)
Work straight for 2 rows.
Next row K2tog, then break off yarn,

thread tail end through rem st and pull to fasten off.

EAR BACKS (MAKE 2)

With 8mm (US size 11) needles and MC, cast on 6 sts.

Beg with a k row, work 2 rows in st st, ending with a p row.

Cont in st st throughout, inc 1 st at each end of next row. (8 sts.)

Work straight for 5 rows, ending with a p row.

Dec 1 st at each end of next row and then at each end of foll alt row, ending with a k row. (4 sts.)

Work straight for 1 row.

Cast off.

Make a second ear back in same way.

EAR FRONTS (MAKE 2)

With 8mm (US size 11) needles and A, cast on 5 sts.

Work 2 rows in garter st.

Cont in garter st throughout, inc 1 st at each end of next row. (7 sts.)

Work straight for 5 rows.

Dec 1 st at each end of next row and then at each end of foll alt row. (3 sts.)

Work straight for 1 row.

Cast off.

Make a second ear front in same way.

TO FINISH

Using double-knitting yarn, sew fronts of ears to backs. Sew ears to mouse's head, parallel to front legs and approximately 7.5cm/3in apart. Lightly press ear backs on wrong side, following instructions on yarn label and avoiding garter st.

Nose, whiskers and eyes

Using a blunt-ended yarn needle and A, sew tip of head over and over to make nose. For whiskers, cut eight 10cm/4in lengths of A. Fold one length in half and use a crochet hook to pull looped end through edge of mat 6mm/1/4in from nose; pull ends of yarn through loop and tighten. Attach three more lengths of yarn A along edge of head and about 12mm/1/2in apart, working away from nose. Attach four whiskers on other side of nose in same way. Sew on two buttons for eyes, about 5cm/2in apart and 4cm/11/2in from ears.

PARTY **DOG** COLLARS

Dress up your dog for a special occasion in a party dog collar. The covers are slipped onto the dog's collar and then popped over its head. There are five designs to choose from: a majestic ruffle, a chic tapestry of flowers, dashing spots, a Hell's Angel collar for the rottweiler in your dog or perhaps a seductive garland of flowers.

RUFFLE **DOG** COLLAR

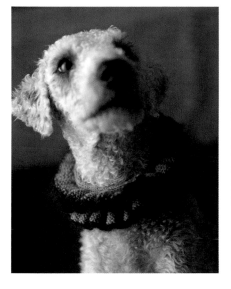

LEVEL
Easy

SIZES
The finished collar cover measures approximately 4cm/1¹/₂in wide for all sizes, and the lengths are as follows:
Extra-extra small – to fit collar size 25cm/10in
Extra small – to fit collar size 30.5cm/12in
Small – to fit collar size 35.5cm/14in
Medium – to fit collar size 40.5cm/16in
Large – to fit collar size 45.5cm/18in
Extra large – to fit collar size 50.5cm/20in

MATERIALS
1 (1: 2: 2: 2: 2) x 50g/1³/₄oz balls of of Jaeger *Matchmaker Merino 4-Ply* in main colour **MC**
1 x 25g/⁷/₈oz ball of Rowan *Kidsilk Haze* in a contrasting colour **A**
Pair of 3.25mm (US size 3) knitting needles

TENSION
28 sts and 36 rows to 10cm/4in measured over st st using 3.25mm (US size 3) needles and MC.

ABBREVIATIONS
See page 17.

TO MAKE COLLAR COVER
With 3.25mm (US size 3) needles and MC, cast on 24 sts.
Work 2 rows in garter st (knit every row).
Beg st st section as follows:
1st row (RS) K6, p1, k17.
2nd row P17, k1, p6.
Rep last 2 rows until collar cover measures 22.5 (28: 33: 38: 43: 48)cm/
9 (11: 13: 15: 17: 19)in from cast-on edge, ending with a WS row.
Work 2 rows in garter st, ending with a WS row.
Next row (RS) Cast off first 12 sts knitwise, k to end. *(12 sts.)*
Work 10 rows in garter st.
Cast off knitwise.

RUFFLE
With 3.25mm (US size 3) needles and A, cast on 165 (195: 231: 267: 306: 363) sts.
Work 2 rows in garter st (knit every row).
Break off A, change to MC and cont as follows:
Work 12 rows in garter st.
Next row *K3tog; rep from * to end.
(55 (65: 77: 89: 102: 121) sts.)
Work 2 rows in garter st.
Next row [K1, p1, k1] all into each st to end (to inc twice into each st).
(165 (195: 231: 267: 306: 363) sts.)
Work 12 rows in garter st.
Break off MC, change to A and cont as follows:

Work 2 rows in garter st.
Cast off knitwise.

TO FINISH
Press collar cover lightly on wrong side, following instructions on yarn label.
With wrong side of ruffle facing right side of collar cover, sew ruffle to collar cover, stitching along centre of ruffle and through line of rev st st on collar cover.
Fold collar cover in half lengthways and sew long side edges together to form a tube.
Sew cast-off edge of collar cover to corresponding section of cast-on edge.
Slip cover onto dog's collar, positioning buckle over garter st section.

FLORAL **DOG** COLLAR

LEVEL
Intermediate

SIZES
The finished collar cover measures approximately 4cm/1½in wide for all sizes, and the lengths are as follows:
Extra small – to fit collar size 30.5cm/12in
Small – to fit collar size 35.5cm/14in
Medium – to fit collar size 40.5cm/16in
Large – to fit collar size 45.5cm/18in
Extra large – to fit collar size 50.5cm/20in

MATERIALS
1 x 50g/1¾oz ball of Jaeger *Matchmaker Merino 4-Ply* in main colour **MC** (charcoal/Anthracite 217), for background
Small amount of Jaeger *Matchmaker Merino 4-Ply* in **A** (light blue/Dewberry), for flower petal motifs
Small amount of Rowan *Scottish Tweed 4-Ply* in each of **B** (blue-green/Sea Green 006), **C** (lavender/Lavender 005) and **D** (green/Apple 015), for leaf motifs and flower centres
Pair of 3.25mm (US size 3) knitting needles

TENSION
28 sts and 36 rows to 10cm/4in measured over st st using 3.25mm (US size 3) needles and MC.
31 rows to 10cm/4in measured over chart patt using 3.25mm (US size 3) needles.

ABBREVIATIONS
See page 17.

CHART NOTE
The chart is worked in st st. When working from the chart, read odd-numbered rows (k rows) from right to left, and even-numbered rows (p rows) from left to right. When working the chart pattern, use the intarsia method (see page 14), knitting with a separate small ball (or long length) of yarn for each area of colour and twisting yarns together on wrong side when changing colour to avoid holes.

TO MAKE COLLAR COVER
With 3.25mm (US size 3) needles and MC, cast on 24 sts.

Work 2 rows in garter st (knit every row).
Beg with a k row, work 0 (2: 10: 20: 28) rows in st st, ending with a WS row.
Beg with a k row and chart row 1, work in st st foll chart (see page 136) until all 98 chart rows have been completed, ending with a p row.
Using MC only and cont in st st, work 0 (2: 10: 20: 28 rows), ending with a p row – collar cover measures 28 (33: 38: 43: 48)cm/11 (13: 15: 17: 19)in from cast-on edge.
Work 2 rows in garter stitch, ending with a WS row.
Next row (RS) Cast off first 12 sts knitwise,

k to end. *(12 sts.)*
Work 10 rows in garter st.
Cast off knitwise.

TO FINISH
Block and press lightly on wrong side, following instructions on yarn label.
Fold collar cover in half lengthways with right sides together and sew long side edges together to form a tube. Turn right side out and press again.
Sew cast-off edge of collar cover to corresponding section of cast-on edge.
Slip cover onto dog's collar, positioning buckle over garter st section.

SPOT **DOG** COLLAR

LEVEL
Easy

SIZES
The finished collar cover measures approximately 4cm/1¹/₂in wide for all sizes, and the lengths are as follows:

Extra-extra small – to fit collar size 25cm/10in
Extra small – to fit collar size 30.5cm/12in
Small – to fit collar size 35.5cm/14in
Medium – to fit collar size 40.5cm/16in
Large – to fit collar size 45.5cm/18in
Extra large – to fit collar size 50.5cm/20in

MATERIALS
1 x 50g/1³/₄oz ball of Jaeger *Matchmaker Merino 4-Ply* (or Rowan *Scottish Tweed 4-Ply*) in main colour **MC**, for background
Small amount of Jaeger *Matchmaker Merino 4-Ply* (or Rowan *Scottish Tweed 4 Ply*) in each of 5 (5: 5: 5: 5: 6) contrasting colours, for spot motifs
Pair of 3.25mm (US size 3) knitting needles

TENSION
28 sts and 36 rows to 10cm/4in measured over st st using 3.25mm (US size 3) needles and MC.

ABBREVIATIONS
See page 17.

CHART NOTE
The chart is worked in st st. When working from the chart, read odd-numbered rows (k rows) from right to left, and even-numbered rows (p rows) from left to right. When working the chart pattern, use the intarsia method (see page 14), knitting with a separate small ball (or long length) of yarn for each area of colour and twisting yarns together on wrong side when changing colour to avoid holes.

TO MAKE COLLAR COVER
With 3.25mm (US size 3) needles and MC, cast on 24 sts.
Work 2 rows in garter st (knit every row).

Beg with a k row, work 4 rows in st st, ending with a p row.
Beg with a k row and chart row 1, work in st st foll chart (see page 136) until all 16 chart rows have been completed, using desired contrasting colour for first spot motif.
Cont as set, repeating chart rows 1–16 and using desired random contrasting colours for spot motifs, until collar cover measures approximately 22.5 (28: 33: 38: 43: 48)cm/9 (11: 13: 15: 17: 19)in from cast-on edge and ending with a chart row 8 (a p row).
Cont with MC only, work 2 rows in garter st, ending with a WS row.

Next row (RS) Cast off first 12 sts knitwise, k to end. *(12 sts.)*
Work 10 rows in garter st.
Cast off knitwise.

TO FINISH
Block and press lightly on wrong side, following instructions on yarn label.
Fold collar cover in half lengthways with right sides together and sew long side edges together to form a tube. Turn right side out and press again.
Sew cast-off edge of collar cover to corresponding section of cast-on edge.
Slip cover onto dog's collar, positioning buckle over garter st section.

HELL'S ANGEL **DOG** COLLAR

LEVEL
Intermediate

SIZES
The finished collar cover measures approximately 4cm/1¹/₂in wide for all sizes, and the lengths are as follows:
Small – to fit collar size 35.5cm/14in
Medium – to fit collar size 40.5cm/16in
Large – to fit collar size 45.5cm/18in
Extra large – to fit collar size 50.5cm/20in

MATERIALS
1 x 50g/1³/₄oz ball of Rowan *4-Ply Soft* in main colour **MC** (black/Black 383), for background
Small amount of Twilleys *Goldfingering* in **A** (gold/Gold 002), for lettering and part of motif
Small amount of Rowan *4-Ply Soft* in each of **B** (white/Nippy 376) and **C** (red/Honk 374), for motifs
Pair of 3.25mm (US size 3) knitting needles

TENSION
28 sts and 36 rows to 10cm/4in measured over st st using 3.25mm (US size 3) needles and MC.

ABBREAVIATIONS
See page 17.

CHART NOTE
The chart is worked in st st. When working from the chart, read odd-numbered rows (k rows) from right to left, and even-numbered rows (p rows) from left to right. When working the chart pattern, use the intarsia method (see page 14), knitting with a separate small ball (or long length) of yarn for each area of colour and twisting yarns together on wrong side when changing colour to avoid holes.

TO MAKE COLLAR COVER
With 3.25mm (US size 3) needles and MC, cast on 24 sts.

Work 2 rows in garter st (knit every row).
Beg with a k row, work 2 (8: 16: 26) rows in st st, ending with a p row.
Beg with a k row and chart row 1, work in st st foll chart (see page 136) until all 106 chart rows have been completed, ending with a p row.
Using MC only and cont in st st, work until collar cover measures 33 (38: 43: 48)cm/ 13 (15: 17: 19)in from cast-on edge, ending with a p row.
Work 2 rows in garter stitch, ending with a WS row.
Next row (RS) Cast off first 12 sts knitwise, k to end. *(12 sts.)*

Work 10 rows in garter st.
Cast off knitwise.

TO FINISH
Block and press lightly on wrong side, following instructions on yarn label.
Fold collar cover in half lengthways with right sides together and sew long side edges together to form a tube. Turn right side out and press again.
Sew cast-off edge of collar cover to corresponding section of cast-on edge.
Slip cover onto dog's collar, positioning buckle over garter st section.

GARLAND **DOG** COLLAR

LEVEL
Intermediate

SIZES
The finished collar cover measures approximately 4cm/1¹/₂in wide for all sizes, and the lengths are as follows:
Extra-extra small – to fit collar size 25cm/10in
Extra-small – to fit collar size 30.5cm/12in
Small – to fit collar size 35.5cm/14in
Medium – to fit collar size 40.5cm/16in
Large – to fit collar size 45.5cm/18in
Extra-large – to fit collar size 50.5cm/20in

MATERIALS
1 x 50g/1³/₄oz ball of Jaeger *Matchmaker Merino 4-Ply* in main colour **MC** (mustard/Gold 756)
1 x 25g/⁷/₈oz ball of Rowan *Scottish Tweed 4-Ply* each in 6 different colours:
A (purple/Thistle 016), **B** (maroon/Claret 013), **C** (blue-green/Sea Green 006), **D** (rust/Rust 009), **E** (lavender/Lavender 005), **F** (green/Apple 015), OR any scraps of leftover 4–ply yarn at hand
Pair of 3.25mm (US size 3) knitting needles

TENSION
28 sts and 36 rows to 10cm/4in measured over st st using 3.25mm (US size 3) needles and MC.

ABBREVIATIONS
See page 17.

TO MAKE COLLAR COVER
With 3.25mm (US size 3) needles and MC, cast on 24 sts.
Work 2 rows in garter st (knit every row).
Beg with a k row, work in st st until collar cover measures 22.5 (28: 33: 38: 43: 48)cm/9 (11: 13: 15: 17: 19)in from cast-on edge, ending with a p row.
Work 2 rows in garter st, ending with a WS row.
Next row (RS) Cast off first 12 sts knitwise, k to end. *(12 sts.)*
Work 10 rows in garter st.
Cast off knitwise.

FLOWER 1
With 3.25mm (US size 3) needles and A, cast on 40 sts.
Knit 1 row.

First petal
Next row (RS) K10, then turn, leaving rem sts unworked.
Working on these 10 sts only, make first petal as follows:
Purl 1 row.
Cont in st st throughout, inc 1 st at each end of next row and at each end of foll alt row, ending with a k row. *(14 sts.)*

Purl 1 row.
Dec 1 st at each end of next row and at each end of every foll alt row until 2 sts rem, ending with a k row.
Next row (WS) P2tog, then break off yarn, thread tail end through rem st and pull tight to fasten off.

Second petal
With RS facing, return to sts left unworked and using D, k10, then turn, leaving rem sts unworked.
Working on these 10 sts only, make second petal as follows:

70

Knit 1 row.

Cont in garter st throughout, inc 1 st at each end of next row and at each end of foll alt row. *(14 sts.)*

Knit 1 row.

Dec 1 st at each end of next row and at each end of every foll alt row until 2 sts rem.

Next row K2tog, then break off yarn, thread tail end through rem st and pull tight to fasten off.

Third and fourth petals

Cont as set, working third petal in st st in A as for first petal and fourth (final) petal in garter st in D as for second petal.

FLOWER 2

With 3.25mm (US size 3) needles and C, cast on 32 sts.

Knit 1 row.

First petal

Next row (RS) K10, then turn, leaving rem sts unworked.

Working on these 10 sts only, make first petal as follows:

Cont in garter st throughout, inc 1 st at each end of next row and at each end of foll alt row. *(14 sts.)*

Dec 1 st at each end of next row and at each end of every foll alt row until 2 sts rem.

Next row K2tog, then break off yarn, thread tail end through rem st and pull tight to fasten off.

Second petal

With RS facing, return to sts left unworked and using D, k6, then turn, leaving rem sts unworked.

Working on these 6 sts only, make second petal as follows:

Purl 1 row.

Cont in st st throughout, inc 1 st at each end of next row and at each end of 2 foll alt rows, ending with a k row. *(12 sts.)*

Purl 1 row.

Work 2 rows in st st, ending with a p row.

Dec 1 st at each end of next row and at each end of every foll alt row until 2 sts rem, ending with a k row.

Next row (WS) P2tog, then break off yarn, thread tail end through rem st and pull tight to fasten off.

Third and fourth petals

Cont as set, working third petal in garter st in C across 10 sts as for first petal and fourth (final) petal in st st in D across 6 sts as for second petal.

STAMENS (MAKE 6)

With 3.25mm (US size 3) needles and E, cast on 14 sts.

Cast off knitwise.

Make 5 more stamens in same way.

(If you want stamens to look particularly botanical, sew over and over end of each stamen to make the stigma, using F.)

LEAVES (MAKE 3)

With 3.25mm (US size 3) needles and F, cast on 5 sts.

1st row (RS) *K1, k into front and back of next st—called *inc into next st*; rep from * once more, k1. *(7 sts.)*

2nd row and all foll WS rows Purl to end.

3rd row K2, inc into next st, k1, inc into next st, k2. *(9 sts.)*

5th row K3, inc into next st, k1, inc into next st, k3. *(11 sts.)*

7th row K4, inc into next st, k1, inc into next st, k4. *(13 sts.)*

9th row K5, inc into next st, k1 inc into next st, k5. *(15 sts.)*

11th row K to end.

13th row K1, k2tog, k9, k2tog, k1. *(13 sts.)*

15th row K1, k2tog, k7, k2tog, k1. *(11 sts.)*

17th row K1, k2tog, k5, k2tog, k1. *(9 sts.)*

19th row K1, k2tog, k3, k2tog, k1. *(7 sts.)*

21st row K1, k2tog, k1, k2tog, k1. *(5 sts.)*

Cast off purlwise.

PETALS (MAKE 2)

With 3.25mm (US size 3) needles and B, cast on 4 sts.

Working in garter st throughout, inc 1 st at each end of first row and at each end of 3 foll alt rows. *(12 sts.)*

Knit 1 row.

Dec 1 st at each end of next row and at each end of 4 foll alt rows. *(2 sts.)*

Knit 1 row.

Next row (RS) K2tog, then break off yarn, thread tail end through rem st and pull tight to fasten off.

Make second petal in same way.

TO FINISH

Press collar cover, leaves and petals lightly on wrong side, following instructions on yarn label.

Fold collar cover in half lengthways with right sides together and sew long side edges together to form a tube. Turn right side out and press again.

Add petals and leaves

Curl flower 1 around on itself and sew together at base so that it forms a four-petalled flower. Sew three stamens to centre of flower.

Sew flower 2 together in same way.

Arrange flowers, leaves and petals at centre of collar as shown, positioning cast-off end of leaves and cast-on end of petals under flowers. Sew in place as arranged.

Sew cast-off edge of collar cover to corresponding section of cast-on edge.

Slip cover onto dog's collar, positioning buckle over garter st section.

TORTOISE HIBERNATION TENT

Why should a tortoise spend six months a year living in a cardboard box? At last: a chance to knit a magnificent tent for your tortoise to winter in. Knitted in subtle colours, the tent will look gorgeous in most places, be it a garden shed or a cellar, but do keep it dry. For the remaining six months, perhaps lend the tent to your cat, small dog or use it for a teddy bear's camping holiday.

TORTOISE HIBERNATION TENT

LEVEL
Knitted tent: Easy
Wooden tent frame: Intermediate

SIZE
The finished tent measures approximately 35cm/14in wide by 48cm/19in long by 37.5cm/15in tall.

MATERIALS
Knitted tent
2 x 50g/1³/₄oz balls of Jaeger *Matchmaker Merino DK* in **A**
(mid blue/Mariner 629), for base of tent
2 x 50g/1³/₄oz balls of Jaeger *Matchmaker Merino DK* in **B**
(lilac/Dusk 626), for one side of tent
2 x 50g/1³/₄oz balls of Jaeger *Matchmaker Merino DK* in **C**
(light sea blue/Marine 914), for one side of tent
1 x 50g/1³/₄oz ball of Jaeger *Matchmaker Merino DK* in **D**
(dark green/Loden 730), for back of tent
1 x 50g/1³/₄oz ball of Jaeger *Matchmaker Merino DK* in **E**
(light green/Sage 857), for front of tent
Pair of 4mm (US size 6) knitting needles
Wooden tent frame
3 lengths of wooden dowelling, each 6mm/¹/₄in in diameter and
approximately 51cm/20in long (to fit along two sides of base of tent and
along top of tent)
2 lengths of wooden dowelling, each 6mm/¹/₄in in diameter and
approximately 40.5cm/16in long (to fit along front and back of base of tent)
4 lengths of wooden dowelling, each 6mm/¹/₄in in diameter and
approximately 48.5cm/19in long (to form A-shape frames at front and
back of tent)
Jute twine or string (a slightly rough version will hold better)
Insulation tape, for binding frame joints

TENSION
22 sts and 30 rows to 10cm/4in measured over st st using 4mm
(US size 6) needles.

ABBREVIATIONS
See page 17.

SPECIAL NOTE
Do not cut the dowelling into pieces for the frame until you have finished knitting
the tent. Because of variable tensions you may need to adjust the length of the
dowelling to fit the size of the finished knitting.

KNITTED TENT

BASE OF TENT

With 4mm (US size 6) needles and A, cast on 106 sts.
1st row (RS) K to end.
2nd row K5, p to end.
Rep last 2 rows (working in st st with a 5-st border in garter st along tent front edge as set) until base measures 35cm/14in from cast-on edge (approximately 104 rows in total), ending with a p row.
Cast off.

LONG SIDE OF TENT (MAKE 2)

With 4mm (US size 6) needles and B, cast on 106 sts.
Beg with a k row, work in st st until side measures 37.5cm/15in from cast-on edge (approximately 112 rows in total), ending with a p row.
Cast off.
Make second side in same way, but using C.

BACK OF TENT

With 4mm (US size 6) needles and D, cast on 80 sts.
Beg with a k row, work 2 rows in st st, ending with a p row.
Cont in st st throughout, dec 1 st at each end of next row and then at each end of every foll 3rd row until 2 sts rem (118 rows in total), ending with a p row.
Next row K2tog, then break off D, thread tail end through rem st and pull tight to fasten off.

RIGHT FRONT OF TENT

With 4mm (US size 6) needles and E, cast on 41 sts.
Work 2 rows in garter st (knit every row).
Cont in garter st, dec 1 st at beg of next row. *(39 sts.)*
Work 1 row more in garter st.
Next row (RS) K to end.
Next row K5, p to last 2 sts, p2tog. *(37 sts.)*
Next row K to end.
Next row K5, p to end.
Cont as set, working in st st with a 5-st border in garter st along left edge, **and at the same time** dec 1 st at beg of next row and at same edge (edge without border) on every foll 3rd row until 2 sts rem, ending with a p row.
Next row K2tog, then break off E, thread tail end through rem st and pull tight to fasten off.

LEFT FRONT OF TENT

With 4mm (US size 6) needles and E, cast on 41 sts.
Work 2 rows in garter st (knit every row).
Cont in garter st, dec 1 st at end of next row. *(39 sts.)*
Work 1 row more in garter st.
Next row (RS) K to end.
Next row P2tog, p to last 5 sts, k5. *(37 sts.)*
Next row K to end.
Next row P to last 5 sts, k5.
Cont as set, working in st st with a 5-st border in garter st along right edge, **and at the same time** dec 1 st at end of next row and at same edge (edge without border) on every foll 3rd row until 2 sts rem, ending with a p row.
Next row K2tog, then break off E, thread tail end through rem st and pull tight to fasten off.

BUNTING

With 4mm needles and A, cast on 116 sts.
Knit 1 row.
Next row (RS) Cast off first 19 sts knitwise, k until there are 8 sts on right needle, then turn, leaving rem sts unworked.
Working on these 8 sts only, drop A and make first flag as follows:
**Using B for flag, work 7 rows in garter st (knit every row).
Cont in garter st for flag throughout, dec 1 st at each end of next row. *(6 sts.)*
Work 7 rows in garter st.
Dec 1 st at each end of next row. *(4 sts.)*
Work 7 rows in garter st.
Next row [K2tog] twice. *(2 sts.)*
Work 1 row in garter st.
Next row K2tog, then break off flag yarn, thread tail end through rem st and pull tight to fasten off.**
With RS facing, return to sts left unworked and using A, cast off 2 sts knitwise, k until there are 8 sts on right needle, then turn, leaving rem sts unworked. Working on these 8 sts only, drop A and make next flag as for first flag from ** to ** but using C.
Rep from *** to *** 6 times more, using D for 3rd flag, E for 4th flag, B for 5th flag, C for for 6th flag, D for 7th flag and E for 8th flag.
With RS facing, return to sts left unworked and using A, cast off rem sts knitwise.

TO FINISH

Block and press tent pieces lightly on wrong side, following instructions on yarn label.
With right sides together, sew cast-on edge of tent base to cast-on edge of side worked in B, and sew cast-off edge of tent base to cast-on edge of side worked in C. Then sew cast-off edges of sides together at top to form a triangular shape.
Sew back of tent to back of base (end without garter st border) and sides, leaving a 2.5cm/1in opening at top for dowelling to stick out of.
Sew fronts together for 2.5cm/1in at centre top, 2.5cm/1in below top edge, so leaving a split at apex for dowelling.

Cords

Make six cords as follows:
Using E, cut two strands of yarn each 37.5cm/14³/₄in long. Holding two strands together, knot each end. Ask a friend to hold one end (or tie one end to a door handle). Insert a pencil in front of knot between two strands at each end and have person at each end twist pencil clockwise until strands are very tightly twisted. Fold twisted yarn in half, give it a slight pull, then allow it to twist up on itself. Smooth out any unevenness, working away from knots. Knot together knotted end, and cut off original two knots. Sew folded (unknotted) end of each cord to centre of borders on tent fronts, stitching three to each front and spacing them evenly apart.

WOODEN TENT FRAME

TO CUT FRAME PIECES

Check that the tent width, length and height match the sizes given at the beginning of the pattern, and adjust the dowelling lengths given in the Materials list if necessary.

Next, cut nine dowelling pieces to the correct lengths with a saw, and gently sand the ends.

TO ASSEMBLE FRAME

Cut the twine into 30.5cm/12in lengths.
(Fig 1) Starting with the base-frame of the tent, use twine to bind together two 51cm/ 20in lengths of dowelling (to fit along the sides of the tent base) with two 40.5cm/16in lengths (to fit along the front and back of the tent base). To bind the dowelling together, wrap the twine over and around the 'joint', leaving about 12mm (1/2in) of the dowelling protruding. Once the joint is fairly secure, knot the twine. (When the tent is finished, the structure will be more stable.)
(Fig 2) Take two 48.5cm/19in lengths of dowelling and bind them together at the top to form an A-shape for the back of the tent, leaving about 5cm/2in above the binding (as on a wigwam) to tie the bunting onto.
(Fig 3) Place the bottom of the A-shape on the inside of the back corners of the base-frame and bind in place with twine. Make a second A-shape frame for the front of the tent, using the remaining two 48.5cm/19in lengths of dowelling; then bind it to the base-frame.
Wrap the tape around the four joints at the base of the tent to stop the dowelling from sliding.

Rest the remaining 51cm/20in length of dowelling in the crosses at the top of A-shapes, and bind in place at each end using twine only.

TO SET UP TENT

(Fig 4) Carefully slip the tent over the frame, allowing the crossed points of dowelling to pass through the openings at the two top corners of the tent.
To secure the bunting to the tent, tie one end to the top of left front dowelling stick and tie the other end to right back dowelling stick. Fill the tent with straw and introduce your tortoise.

ANTI-FIREWORK **DOG** BALACLAVA

This is a really useful item for all those dogs that find fireworks a misery. Just slip on the balaclava, with extra earmuff protection, and your dog's ears are muffled from the terrifying sounds. As you can see they also cut quite a dash.

ANTI-FIREWORK **DOG** BALACLAVA

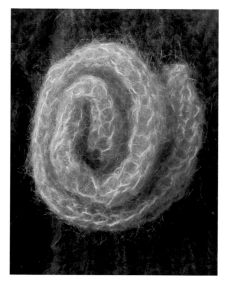

LEVEL
Easy

SIZES
Small – to fit small to medium-size dog
The finished small size measures
approximately 24cm/9^1/2in around
the neck and 26.5cm/10^1/2in long
unstretched.
Large – to fit medium-size to large dog
The finished large size measures
approximately 32cm/12^1/2in around
the neck and 30.5cm/12in long
unstretched.
Note: The ribbed balaclava is stretchy
and will fit easily over the dog's head;
when on the dog, the circumference
will be wider and the length shorter
than when unstretched.

MATERIALS
1 (2) x 50g/1^3/4oz ball of Rowan
Kid Classic in main colour **MC**,
for balaclava
Small amount of Rowan *Kidsilk Haze*
in a contrasting colour **A**, for earmuffs
Pair of 5mm (US size 8) knitting needles

TENSION
18–19 sts and 23–25 rows to
10cm/4in measured over st st using
5mm (US size 8) knitting needles
and MC.

ABBREVIATIONS
See page 17.

TO MAKE BALACLAVA
With 5mm (US size 8) needles and MC,
cast on 62 (82) sts.
Beg k2, p2 rib as follows:
1st rib row (RS) *K2, p2; rep from * to
last 2 sts, k2.
2nd rib row *P2, k2; rep from * to last
2 sts, p2.
(Last 2 rows are repeated to form k2,
p2 rib patt.)
Work 38 (44) rows more in k2, p2 rib,
ending with a WS row.

Divide for front opening
Keeping rib patt correct as set, divide for
opening on next row as follows:
Next row (RS) Work first 25 (32) sts in
rib and slip these sts onto a st holder, then
cast off next 12 (18) sts in rib, work in
rib to end.
Working on these 25 (32) sts only, cont
as follows:
Work 15 (19) rows in rib, ending with
a WS row.
Break off MC and leave these sts on
a spare needle.
With WS facing, rejoin MC to sts on
holder and work in rib to end.
Work 14 (18) rows in rib, ending with
a WS row.
Next row (RS) Work in rib across 25 (32)
on needle, cast on 12 (18) sts onto right-
hand needle, then work in rib across 25
(32) sts on spare needle. *(62 (82) sts.)*
Work 1 row in rib.

Shape top
Next row (RS) *K6, k2tog; rep from * to
last 6 (2) sts, k6 (2). *(55 (72) sts.)*

Purl 1 row.
Next row *K5, k2tog; rep from * to last
6 (2) sts, k6 (2). *(48 (62) sts.)*
Purl 1 row.
Next row *K4, k2tog; rep from * to last
6 (2) sts, k6 (2). *(41 (52) sts.)*
Purl 1 row.
Next row *K3, k2tog; rep from * to last
6 (2) sts, k6 (2). *(34 (42) sts.)*
Purl 1 row.
Next row *K2, k2tog; rep from * to last
6 (2) sts, k6 (2). *(27 (32) sts.)*
Purl 1 row.
Next row [K2tog] 13 (16) times, k1 (0).
(14 (16) sts.)
Next row [P2tog] 7 (8) times. *(7 (8) sts.)*
Next row [K2tog] 3 (4) times, k1 (0).
(4 sts.)
Next row [P2tog] twice. *(2 sts.)*
Next row K2tog, then break off MC,
thread tail end through rem st and pull
tight to fasten off.

EARMUFFS (MAKE 2)
With 5mm (US size 8) needles and A,
cast on 10 sts.
Beg with a k row, work in st st until strip
measures 25cm/10in from cast-on edge,
ending with a WS row.
Cast off, leaving a long tail end.

TO FINISH
Press balaclava very lightly on WS,
following instructions on yarn label.
Sew side edges of balaclava together
to form back seam.

Earmuffs
Do not press earmuff strips, but allow them
to curl in along side edges to form a long
tube shape. Starting at cast-on end, curl
each strip into a spiralling circle (like a
snail), about 6.5cm/2^1/2in in diameter.
Thread long tail end onto a blunt-ended
yarn needle and secure circle shape by
passing needle through circle spirals from
one edge of circle to opposite edge.
Sew one earmuff to each side of balaclava,
level with centre of front opening.

BUDGIE BLANKET

For the discerning bird, a knitted cage cover. As they sit on their perch and look up they will have the illusion that they are gazing up at the sky through a canopy of leaves. They may of course not notice this feature, but as they sleep you will have the added bonus of a beautiful piece of knitting to admire.

BUDGIE BLANKET

LEVEL
Intermediate

SIZE
The finished blanket measures approximately 59cm/23¼in wide by 137cm/54in long.
Note: To make the blanket longer, you can add rows in MC before beginning the chart and the same number of rows in MC after completing the chart. To make the blanket wider, add the same number of stitches to each side of chart in MC.

MATERIALS
5 x 50g/1¾oz balls of Jaeger *Matchmaker Merino DK* in main colour **MC** (dark olive), for borders and outer background
3 x 50g/1¾oz ball of Jaeger *Matchmaker Merino DK* in **E** (pale blue), for centre background
1 x 50g/1¾oz ball of Jaeger *Matchmaker Merino DK* in each of **A** (mid green), **B** (pale lime green), **C** (light green), **D** (dark green) and **F** (brown), for leaf motifs
Pair of 4mm (US size 6) knitting needles

TENSION
22 sts and 30 rows to 10cm/4in measured over st st using 4mm (US size 6) needles.

ABBREVIATIONS
See page 17.

CHART NOTE
The chart is worked in st st. When working from the chart, read odd-numbered rows (k rows) from right to left, and even-numbered rows (p rows) from left to right. When working the chart pattern, use the intarsia method (see page 14), knitting with a separate small ball (or long length) of yarn for each area of colour and twisting yarns together on wrong side when changing colour to avoid holes.
Note: The chart shows only the st st section of the blanket; the garter stitch borders are not included on the chart.

TO MAKE BLANKET
With 4mm (US size 6) needles and MC, cast on 130 sts.
Work 10 rows in garter st (knit every row).
Beg st st patt with garter st borders for centre of cover as follows:
Next row (RS) Knit.
Next row K10, p110, k10.
Rep last 2 rows 18 times more, ending with a WS row.
Set position of chart patt (see pages 138–139) on next 2 rows as follows:
Next row (RS) K10; k next 110 sts foll chart row 1; k10.
Next row K10; p next 110 sts foll chart row 2; k10.
Cont foll chart as set and working 10-st garter st borders until all 162 rows of chart have been completed, ending with a WS row.
Then turn chart upside down and cont in patt by working all 162 rows in opposite direction – a total of 324 chart rows in total, ending with a WS row.
Using MC only for remainder of cover, work 38 rows in st st with 10-st garter st borders.
Work 10 rows in garter st.
Cast off knitwise.

TO FINISH
Block and press cover lightly on wrong side, following instructions on yarn label and avoiding garter st borders.

ROSETTE

If you or your pet are feeling unrewarded in the
gymkhana of life, why not knit your own rosette?
You can leave it plain or embroider whatever you
like in the centre: 1st Prize, Runner-up, Best in Show…
the choice is up to you, but there's not much room,
so make it short.

ROSETTE

LEVEL
Easy

SIZE
The finished rosette with pleated border measures approximately 12cm/4³/₄in in diameter and the tails measure approximately 12.5cm/5in and 15.5cm/6in long.

MATERIALS
1 x 50g/1³/₄oz ball of Rowan *Pure Wool DK* in main colour **MC**, for rosette
Small amount of Rowan *Pure Wool DK* in a contrasting colour **A**, for edging
Pair of 4mm (US size 6) knitting needles
Small piece of cardboard, to stiffen rosette centre
Safety pin

TENSION
22 sts and 30 rows to 10cm/4in measured over st st using 4mm (US size 6) needles.

ABBREVIATIONS
See page 17.

ROSETTE CENTRE
With 4mm (US size 6) needles and MC, cast on 10 sts.
Beg with a k row, work 2 rows in st st, ending with a p row.
Cont in st st throughout, inc 1 st at each end of next row and then at each end of 3 foll alt rows, ending with a k row. *(18 sts.)*
Work straight in st st for 10 rows, ending with a k row.
Dec 1 st at each end of next row and then at each end of 3 foll alt rows, ending with a p row. *(10 sts.)*
Work straight for 2 rows. Cast off.

PLEAT STRIP
With 4mm (US size 6) needles and MC, cast on 120 sts.

For pleat with plain edging only
Beg with a k row, work 8 rows in st st, ending with a p (WS) row.

For pleat with a seeded edging only
Beg with a k row, work 7 rows in st st, ending with a k (RS) row.

For both versions
Break off MC and change to A.
Knit 1 row.
Cast off knitwise.

SHORT TAIL
With 4mm (US size 6) needles and MC, cast on 8 sts. Work in garter st (knit every row) until tail measures 10cm/4in from cast-on edge.
**Divide tail
Before beg next row to divide tail, mark this side of work as RS, using a coloured thread.

Next row (RS) K4, then turn, leaving rem sts on a st holder.
Working on these 4 sts only, cont as follows:
Next row (WS) K2tog, k2. *(3 sts.)*
Knit 1 row.
Next row K2tog, k1. *(2 sts.)*
Knit 1 row.
Next row K2tog, then break off MC, thread tail end through rem st and pull tight to fasten off.
With RS facing, rejoin MC to 4 sts on st holder and k to end.
Next row (WS) K2, k2tog. *(3 sts.)*
Knit 1 row
Next row K1, k2tog. *(2 sts.)*
Knit 1 row.
Next row K2tog, then break off MC, thread tail end through rem st and pull tight to fasten off.

LONG TAIL
With 4mm (US size 6) needles and MC, cast on 8 sts.
Work in garter st (knit every row) until tail measures 15cm/6in from cast-on edge.
Complete as for short tail from **.

TO FINISH
Do not press.
Cut a circle of cardboard 6cm/2³/₈in in diameter. Place cardboard circle on wrong side of knitted rosette centre. Then using a blunt-ended yarn needle and a strand of MC, weave yarn in and out around edge of rosette centre; pull tight to gather edge and enclose cardboard inside knitting, and fasten off. Using MC, sew safety pin to back of rosette centre (over top of gathered edge).

Pleated border
Fold pleat strip into approximately 4-stitch pleats along cast-on edge (so that it will fit around rosette centre), and sew pleats in place using MC. Using mattress stitch, sew ends of pleated strip together to form a ring. Sew pleated ring to back of rosette centre, close to edge. Sew cast-on ends of tails (one on top of the other and with short tail to front) to wrong side of lower edge of rosette centre.

ECO-DOG COATS

These are to inspire you to transform your favourite old jumper into a beautiful and completely individual coat for your dog. If, however, you want to keep your beloved old jumper for yourself, charity shops and jumble sales are a rich source of second-hand knitwear. These are ideas that you can elaborate on in your own unique way.

TWINSET AND PEARLS
DOG COAT

LEVEL
Easy

SIZE
The coat is made to fit your dog. It fits around the dog's body, buttons along the dog's belly and has two legs for the dog's front legs.

MATERIALS
One old roundneck wool cardigan, and matching sewing thread
Small amount of black 4-ply or double-knitting wool yarn
Disappearing fabric marker, to mark seams
20 large fake pearls with large holes (holes large enough for a blunt-ended tapestry needle and yarn to pass through)

CHOOSE AND 'FELT' THE OLD CARDIGAN
For this design, we used a traditional long-sleeved wool stocking stitch cardigan, with a petersham ribbon backing along the button and buttonhole bands.
A shrunken sweater or one with holes is ideal and it must be made of pure wool because it needs to be 'felted' in a washing machine. Felting the jumper makes it easier to work with; you can cut straight into it without fear of fraying edges or running stitches.
Wash the jumper with some detergent on a non-colourfast wash at 40°C/105°F. It will come out much smaller and will have a slight cardboard feel. Once dried it will be more pliable.

TO MAKE THE COAT
Measure your dog as explained on page 10 to make sure the felted cardigan is big enough to be cut down to fit your dog.

(Fig 1) Then cut the sleeves off the old felted cardigan in a straight line from the underarm, and perpendicular to the sleeve

seam, so that the sleeve forms a cap. Cut the cuffs off the bottom of the sleeves, including about 1cm/³⁄8in of stocking stitch above them.

Customising to fit your dog
Catch your dog and slip the cardigan on him/her.
(Fig 2) Carefully pin a dart from the neck down the shoulder and onto the cap sleeve to reduce the width of the armhole – you may need to remove up to 3.5cm/1¹⁄2in of knitted fabric. Then pin along the dog's back, taking up most of the excess knitted fabric.
Use a disappearing fabric marker to mark along the seam lines and remove the pins. Take the cardigan off the dog, turn it inside out and pin along the marked lines at the shoulders and along the back. Baste the seams and remove the pins.

Sewing seams
Using a sewing machine – but if you prefer, hand sewing would be fine – stitch along these basted lines. Try the coat on your dog again and make any adjustments. Once satisfied, remove the basting, trim the seams and turn the cardigan right side out. Overlock or zigzag stitch along the edges of the sleeves. Slip the stocking stitch top of the cuff inside the end of the sleeve and sew the cuff to the sleeve, using a blunt-ended tapestry needle, black wool yarn and decorative running stitches. Trim off the excess knitted fabric at the top of the cuff inside the coat.

TO APPLY FINISHING TOUCHES
Using a blunt-ended tapestry needle, black wool yarn and running stitches, start at the button band and sew the pearls to the neck along the base of the neck ribbing. For a decorative effect, make one running stitch in between each pearl. Press and dress.

SILHOUETTE **DOG** COAT

LEVEL
Easy

SIZE
The coat is made to fit your dog. It fits around the dog's body, opens along the dog's belly, has two legs for the dog's front legs, buttons at the front of the dog and is held in place by a belt.

MATERIALS
One old V-neck wool jumper
Piece of an old jumper in a contrasting colour and matching sewing thread, for appliqué
Small amount of black 4-ply or double-knitting wool yarn, for edging
2 buttons

CHOOSE AND PREPARE THE OLD JUMPER
The jumper used for this design was a long-sleeved wool stocking stitch V-neck jumper with fine stripes. The belt was cut from one of the sleeves.
Felt the jumper (and a piece of an old jumper in a contrasting colour for the appliqué), as explained on page 93 before beginning the coat.

TO MAKE THE COAT
Measure your dog as explained on page 10 to make sure the old felted jumper is big enough to be cut down to fit your dog. Then cut the sleeves off the old felted jumper in a straight line from the underarm, and perpendicular to the sleeve seam, so that the sleeve forms a cap. (Save the sleeves to make the belt.)
Cut in a straight line from the point of the V-neck shaping down the centre front.

Customising to fit your dog
Slip the jumper on your dog, with his/her front legs in the sleeves and the newly cut front opening hanging under the dog's body. Depending on the size of the jumper and your dog, you will need to trim off some excess fabric along the front edges of the cardigan. Carefully pin a dart from the neck down the shoulder and onto the cap sleeve to reduce the width of the armhole. You may also need to take out excess fabric down the centre back. If so, pin along here as well.
Use a disappearing fabric marker to mark along the seam lines and remove the pins. Take the jumper off the dog, turn it inside out and pin along the marked seam/dart lines. Baste the seams and remove the pins.

Sewing seams
Using a sewing machine – but if you prefer, hand sewing would be fine – stitch along these basted lines.
Try the coat on your dog again and make any adjustments. Once satisfied, remove the basting, trim the seams and turn the jumper right side out.

To prepare the belt
Measure around the dog's chest. Add an extra 5cm/2in to this measurement for the overlap at the fastening.
Cut a 5cm/2in wide strip for the belt from one of the sleeves of the felted jumper, trying to incorporate the jumper ribbing at one end of the belt. If you want ribbing at each end of the belt, cut half of the belt from each sleeve and sew the strips together at the centre of the belt.

TO APPLY FINISHING TOUCHES
Cut a 12mm/½in slit for the buttonhole on one of the right front just below the jumper neck ribbing and 12mm/½in in from the front edge. Test the size of the buttonhole slit with the button and increase the length if necessary. Then, using a blunt-ended tapestry needle and black yarn, blanket stitch around the buttonhole.
Sew a button to the other side of the front opening.
Work a blanket stitch edging along the front edges of the coat, and then around the ends of the sleeves.

Appliqué
Enlarge a dog silhouette (see page 141 for a choice of templates) by 300–400% using a photocopier. Cut out the shape from the photocopy, pin it to the contrasting piece of felted knitting and cut out the appliqué.
Pin the appliqué to the back of the dog coat, either along the side or across the back. Then using a matching thread, machine zigzag stitch the appliqué in place around the edge. (Alternatively, stitch the appliqué in place by hand with running stitches, using a blunt-ended tapestry needles and a contrasting yarn.)

Belt fastening
For the belt fastening, make a buttonhole as before, 2.5cm/1in from one end of the belt, and sew a button to the other end. Press and dress.

J E W E L L E D **D O G** C O A T

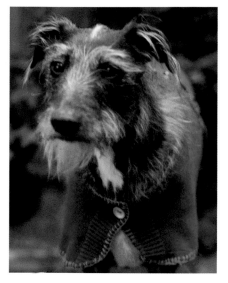

LEVEL
Easy

SIZE
The coat is made to fit your dog. It fits across the dog's back, hangs down the dog's sides, buttons at the front of the dog and is held in place by a belt.

MATERIALS
One old roundneck wool jumper
Remnant of cotton fabric or calico, or a sheet of newspaper, for 'toile' pieces
Small amount of double-knitting wool yarn in a contrasting colour, for edging
Assortment of sew-on jewels
2 buttons

CHOOSE AND PREPARE THE OLD JUMPER
The jumper used for this design was a simple roundneck, long-sleeved, stocking stitch wool jumper. We used the back and front for the body of the coat and one sleeve for the belt.
Felt the cardigan as explained on page 93 before beginning the coat.

TO MAKE THE 'TOILE'
(Fig 1) This coat needs a pattern piece or 'toile' as a guide to cutting the pieces from the old felted jumper.
Measure your dog as explained on page 10.
Using the measurements you have taken from you dog as your guide, draw the shape of half of the coat on a piece of old material or calico – or if nothing else is available, a sheet of newspaper. The seam runs down the centre of the dog's back, so halve the dog's neck and shoulder measurements and allow 6mm/1/4in extra for the centre back seam allowance.
Draw a concave curve from the centre back at the neck edge to the front edge of the coat, for the neck opening and the section that wraps around the front of the dog. (The two front extensions should

overlap about 3cm/1 1/4in at the front of the dog.)
Draw a 5cm/2in wide strip for the belt, long enough to fit around the dog's chest and overlap about 3cm/1 1/4in.
Cut out the 'toile' pieces and try them on the dog, then make any necessary adjustments.

TO MAKE THE COAT
Cut the sleeves off the old felted jumper at the armholes, lay out the jumper flat and place the coat 'toile' on top. It is a good idea to try to incorporate the jumper ribbing either at the front edge of the dog's coat or at the tail-end edge of the coat, or both. Cutting around the 'toile', cut out two pieces from the jumper for the coat.
Using the belt 'toile', cut the belt from one sleeve of the jumper, again trying to incorporate the jumper ribbing at one end of the belt.

Sewing seam
Pin the two sides of the coat together along the centre back, with the wrong sides together. With a contrasting yarn and a blunt-ended tapestry needle, sew the seam using blanket stitches 6mm/1/4in long. Try the coat on your dog again and make any final adjustments.

TO APPLY FINISHING TOUCHES
Cut a 12mm/1/2in slit for the buttonhole on one of the front extensions of the coat, 2.5cm/1in down from the neck edge and 12mm/1/2in in from the front edge. Test the size of the buttonhole slit with the button and increase the length if necessary. Then, using the contrasting yarn, blanket stitch around the buttonhole. Sew a button to the other side of the front opening.
Work a blanket stitch edging all around the outer edge of the coat, and then around the belt.
For the belt fastening, make a buttonhole as before, 12mm/1/2in from one end of the belt. Sew a button to the other end. Decorate the belt with sew-on jewels (available from major craft shops).
Press and dress.

POMPOMS

Very easy to make – you probably know how to already – but in case you have forgotten here are some pompoms to entertain your cat, dog, rat, ferret, snake – everyone enjoys a pompom. Ours are made from wool and a carrier bag, but you can use string, raffia, ribbon, spaghetti – anything you like really. Hours of fun for you and your pet.

POMPOMS

LEVEL
Easy

SIZE
The finished pompoms measure approximately 7.5cm/3in in diameter.
Note: To alter the size of the pompoms, cut smaller or larger cardboard circles.

MATERIALS
Wool pompom
Assorted colours of double-knitting-weight yarn
Plastic pompom
One clear or coloured plastic bag, to make 'yarn'
Both pompoms
Cardboard – a cereal packet is ideal

WOOL POMPOM

CARDBOARD POMPOM TEMPLATES (MAKE 2)
Using a compass or drawing around the base of a mug, draw a circle about 7.5cm/3in in diameter on the cardboard (the size of the circle will be the size of finished pompom). Draw a 2.5cm/1in circle in the centre of the first circle. Cut out the larger circle, then cut out the small circle at the centre.
Make a second cardboard circle exactly the same.

TO MAKE POMPOM
Hold the two cardboard circles together and wind the yarn around the ring as evenly as possible until the hole is almost closed up with yarn (it is quicker to wind several strands at once). Then thread yarn onto a needle and continue to wind until the hole is closed up.
Cut the yarn around the edge of the circles, sliding a point of the scissors along in between the two pieces of cardboard. Ease the cardboard templates slightly apart and wrap a long length of doubled yarn between the templates and around the centre of the pompom. Tie the pompom together tightly at the centre, leaving two long tail ends of yarn hanging.
Then pull, or cut, the cardboard away from the pompom.

Fluff up the pompom and trim into shape if necessary. For a hanging cord, twist the two long ends of yarn together and knot.

PLASTIC POMPOM

TO PREPARE PLASTIC 'YARN'
Prepare the plastic 'yarn' as for the Water Lily on page 52.

TO MAKE POMPOM
Make the cardboard templates and the pompom as for the wool pompom, but be careful not to tear the plastic 'yarn' and use ordinary yarn to tie the pompom at the centre.

PUPPY PAPOOSE

This is a truly indispensable accessory for the pet lover. If you have a small puppy or tiny dog, you will inevitably spend a lot of the time carrying it around. The solution is a soft, comfortable cradle worn close to you. It will keep your puppy feeling warm and secure.

PUPPY PAPOOSE

LEVEL
Intermediate

SIZES
Small – for a young puppy
The finished small size measures approximately 36cm/14in across the widest part and 38.5cm/15in long.
Large – for an older puppy or a small dog
The finished large size measures approximately 41cm/16in across the widest part and 45cm/17¾in long.

MATERIALS
3 x 50g/1¾oz balls of Rowan *Kid Classic* in main colour **MC**
1 x 50g/1¾oz ball of Rowan *Kid Classic* in first contrasting colour **A**, for roses
1 x 50g/1¾oz ball of Rowan *Kid Classic* in second contrasting colour **B**, for leaves and stems
Pair of 4mm (US size 6) knitting needles
Pair of 3.75mm (US size 5) knitting needles
2m/2¼yd of 5cm/2in satin ribbon, for backing the straps
50cm/18in of mattress ticking (or other strong, tightly woven fabric), for lining the papoose
Matching sewing thread, for sewing on ribbon and making lining

TENSION
24 sts and 30 rows to 10cm/4in over st st using 4mm (US size 6) needles.
(**Note:** This needle size is smaller than the size recommended on the yarn label, as it needs to be knitted tightly to help support the weight of the dog.)

ABBREVIATIONS
See page 17.

CHART NOTE
The chart is worked in st st. When working from the chart, read odd-numbered rows (k rows) from right to left, and even-numbered rows (p rows) from left to right. When working the chart pattern, use the intarsia method (see page 14), knitting with a separate small ball (or long length) of yarn for each area of colour and twisting yarns together on wrong side when changing colour to avoid holes.
Note: The chart shows only the st st section of the papoose; the moss stitch borders are not included on the chart.

TO MAKE PAPOOSE
With 4mm (US size 6) needles and MC, cast on 13 sts.
Knit 1 row.
Next row [K1, p1, k1] all into each st to end (to inc twice into each st). *(39 sts.)*
Beg st st patt with moss st borders as follows:
Next row (RS) K1, [p1, k1] twice for moss st border; k into front and back of next st, k to last 6 sts, k into front and back of next st; [k1, p1] twice, k1 for moss st border.
Next row K1, [p1, k1] twice for moss st border; p into front and back of next st, p to last 6 sts, p into front and back of next st; [k1, p1] twice, k1 for moss st border.
Rep last 2 rows twice more. *(51 sts.)*
Set position of chart patt (see page 137) on next 2 rows (chart rows 7 and 8) as follows:
Next row (RS) Using MC moss st 5 sts; using MC k into front and back of next st,

k29MC, k1A, k9MC, using MC k into front and back of next st; using MC moss st 5 sts.
Next row Using MC moss st 5 sts; using MC p into front and back of next st, p9MC, p1A, p31MC, using MC p into front and back of next st; using MC moss st 5 sts.
Cont foll chart as set and working 5-st moss st borders in MC throughout **and at the same time** inc 1 st at each end (inside moss st borders) of next 6 (10) rows, ending with a WS row. *(67 (75) sts.)*
Work 1 row without shaping.
Inc 1 st at each end of next row and then at each end of every foll alt row 9 (11) times, ending with a RS row. *(87 (99) sts.)*
Omitting incomplete motifs on smaller size throughout, work straight until chart row 78 (90) has been completed, ending with a WS row.
Dec 1 st at each end of next row and then at each end of every foll alt row 10 (12) times, ending with a RS row. *(65 (73) sts.)*
Dec 1 st at each end of next 13 (17) rows (cont with MC only after last motif has been completed), ending with a WS row. *(39 sts.)*
Knit 1 row.
Next row (WS) [K3tog] 13 times. *(13 sts.)*
Leave sts on a spare needle.

STRAPS (WORK 2)
Work a strap at each end of papoose as follows:

Strap 1
With RS facing and using 3.75mm (US size 5) needles and MC, work moss st across 13 sts on spare needle as follows:
1st row (RS) *K1, p1; rep from * to last st, k1.
Rep last row until moss st strap measures 51.5cm/20in.

Shape top of strap
Keeping moss st correct as set, dec 1 st at beg of next row and than at same edge of every row 11 times in all. *(2 sts.)*
Next row K2tog, break off MC, thread tail end through rem st and pull to fasten off.

Strap 2
For second strap, with RS facing and using 3.75mm (US size 5) needles and MC, pick up and knit 13 sts along cast-on edge of papoose.
Work in moss st as for first strap until strap measures 66.5cm/26in.
Keeping moss st correct as set, dec 1 st at beg of next row and than at same edge of every row 11 times in all. *(2 sts.)*
Next row K2tog, break off MC, thread tail end through rem st and pull to fasten off.

TO FINISH
Press lightly on wrong side, following instructions on yarn label.

Backing on straps
Cut a piece of ribbon to line each strap, allowing extra at ends for hems. Fold under ends of each length of ribbon, and pin and sew to wrong side of straps, using a sewing machine or handsewing with slip stitches. This ribbon backing will hold straps firm and prevent them from stretching.
Press straps lightly again.

Lining on papoose
Following measurements given in the diagrams below, draw an outline of the lining for the small **(Fig 1)** or large size

(Fig 2) on a piece of newspaper. Then add an extra 1.5cm/½in all around the edge for a hem allowance. Fold newspaper lining pattern in half and cut it out around the outline.
Fold lining fabric in half and pin folded pattern piece on top of it. Then cut the fabric out around paper pattern.
Using a sewing machine, work long, loose gathering stitches along top of lining about 12mm/³⁄₈in from edge, starting at bottom of curve where broken line crosses outline on one side (9cm/3½in down from top) and ending at same place on other side of top. Work gathering stitches along bottom of lining in same way.
Pull gathering stitches on top of lining to gather fabric so that it fits across top of knitted papoose piece. Fold 1.5cm/½in to wrong side long this gathered edge so that gathering stitches are on wrong side of lining, pin and baste. Stitch this hem in place and remove basting.
Gather and stitch bottom edge of lining in same way.
Fold 1.5cm/½in to wrong side along side edges of lining, press and stitch in place.
Pin gathered edges of lining to top and bottom ends of papoose and sew in place. Leave long, straight side edges of lining loose.

HAMSTER HOUSE

A collaborative housing project for you and your
rodent. No more living in a cardboard box
or shapeless ball of sawdust-covered fluff. In no time
at all you can knit your hamster a magnificent new
house. And if your hamster feels inclined, he can
then recycle it into a bed of his own design.

HAMSTER HOUSE

LEVEL
Easy

SIZE
The finished hamster house measures approximately 29.5cm/11³⁄₄in in circumference by 11.5cm/4¹⁄₂in tall, not including tassel at top.

MATERIALS
1 x 100g/3¹⁄₂oz ball of Rowan *Scottish Tweed Aran* in main colour **MC**, for house
Small amount of a 4-ply yarn in a contrasting colour **A**, for tassel
Pair of 3.75mm (US size 5) knitting needles
Crochet hook, for attaching tassel

TENSION
19 sts and 27 rows to 10cm/4in measured over st st using 3.75mm (US size 5) needles.
Note: The house is knitted tighter than suggested on the yarn label so that it is firm enough to stand up.

ABBREVIATIONS
See page 17.

TO MAKE HOUSE
With 3.75mm (US size 5) needles and MC, cast on 56 sts.
Work 6 rows in garter stitch (knit every row).
Mark each end of last row with a coloured thread.
Cont in garter st, cast off 3 sts at beg of each of next 2 rows, then 2 sts at beg of 2 foll rows. (46 sts.)
Work straight in garter st for 6 rows.
Cont in garter st, cast on 2 sts at beg of each of next 2 rows, then 3 sts at beg of 2 foll rows. (56 sts.)
Mark each end of last row with a coloured thread.
Work straight in garter st for 8 rows.

Shape top
Change to st st and shape top of house

as follows:
Next row (RS) [K2tog, k5] 8 times. *(48 sts.)*
Purl 1 row.
Next row [K2tog, k4] 8 times. *(40 sts.)*
Purl 1 row.
Next row [K2tog, k3] 8 times. *(32 sts.)*
Purl 1 row.
Next row [K2tog, k2] 8 times. *(24 sts.)*
Purl 1 row.
Next row [K2tog, k1] 8 times. *(16 sts.)*
Purl 1 row.
Next row [K2tog] 8 times. *(8 sts.)*
Purl 1 row.
Next row [K2tog] 4 times. *(4 sts.)*
Purl 1 row.
Next row [K2tog] twice. *(2 sts.)*
Next row P2tog, then break off MC, thread tail end through rem st and pull tight to fasten off.

TO FINISH
Do not press.
Join house at centre front to form it into a circle as follows:
With right sides together, sew together side edges of knitting between cast-on edge and first set of markers; then sew together side edges of knitting between second set of markers and top point of house. Turn right side out.

Tassel
Cut five strands of A, each 10cm/4in long. Holding strands together, fold them in half and use a crochet hook to pull loop at folded end of strands through top of house. Still using hook, pull ends of strands through loop, then pull ends tight to secure tassel in place.
Trim ends of tassel to desired length.

WIRE **BIRD** FEEDER

Hardly pets, I know, but a crucial part of the animal world, and it is well worth the effort to knit this bird feeder. For the enterprising this is an opportunity to increase your knitting skills, a treat for you and the wild birds in your garden.

WIRE **BIRD** FEEDER

LEVEL
Difficult until you have mastered knitting with wire, then intermediate

SIZE
The finished bird feeder measures approximately 8.5cm/3¼in in diameter by 25.5cm/10in long.

MATERIALS
58m/64yd of 0.5mm wire **A** in silver (either artistic, 15 amp fuse wire, or lacemakers' wire), for bird feeder
19m/21yd of 0.5mm wire **B** in brass, for bird
1m/1yd of 1.00mm wire **C** in silver, for bird feeder handle
Pair of 3.75mm (US size 5) knitting needles
Pair of 3mm (US size 3) knitting needles
Blunt-ended tapestry needle, for sewing seams with wire
Tough scissors or pliers, for cutting and twisting wire
2 lengths of wooden dowelling, 9mm in diameter and 15cm/6in long, OR 2 sticks from garden

TENSION
Approximately 16 sts and 20 rows to 10cm/4in measured over garter st using 3.75mm (US size 5) needles and wire A.

ABBREVIATIONS
See page 17.

TIPS FOR KNITTING WITH WIRE
Knitting with wire can be a little harsh on your hands, but persevere as it is very rewarding. If you have never knit with wire before, here are a few hints that will make it easier:
• Do not use your best needles – we use old aluminium ones.
• Because wire has no stretch, all stitches need to be worked loosely so that you can easily slip the needle into the loops.
• Cast on using the simplest method – the 'backward through loop' cast-on (also called 'thumb' cast-on). To cast on with this method, hold the wire in your right hand and wrap it over your left thumb clockwise and around so it crosses over itself. Next, insert the knitting needle into the loop from below and slip the loop off your thumb; make sure the new cast-on loop now on the right needle is loose. Wrap the wire around your thumb again, but this time without making a crossed loop; then insert the needle into the loop from below and slip the loop onto the needle. Continue adding loops in this way.
• Garter stitch is the best stitch to use with wire because of the effect achieved. It has more bounce and is easy to work.
• Wire has almost no weight and the stitches don't 'drop' naturally as you knit, so about every two rows pull on the knitting to stretch it downwards.
• To increase in the middle of a row, make a yarn-over (yfwd). To increase at the beginning or end of a row, cast on a stitch.
• Always cast off knitwise.

MAIN SECTION OF BIRD FEEDER
With 3.75mm (US size 5) needles and wire A, cast on 40 sts, using 'backward loop' cast-on (see left)
Work 11 rows in garter st (knit every row). Working in garter st throughout, cont as follows:
Next row K5, k2tog, k18, k2tog, k13.
Next row K14, yfwd, k18, yfwd, k6.

Work straight for 17 rows.
Next row K13, k2tog, k18, k2tog, k5.
Next row K6, yfwd, k18, yfwd, k14.
Work straight for 19 rows (a total of 51 rows worked from cast-on edge).
Cast off loosely knitwise.

CIRCULAR BASE OF BIRD FEEDER
With 3.75mm (US size 5) needles and wire A, cast on 6 sts.
Work 2 rows in garter st.
Working in garter st throughout, cont as follows:
Inc 1 st at each end of next row and then at each end of 4 foll alt rows. *(16 sts.)*
Work straight for 6 rows
Dec 1 st at each end of next row and then at each end of 4 foll alt rows. *(6 sts.)*
Work straight for 2 rows.
Cast off loosely knitwise.

CIRCULAR LID OF BIRD FEEDER
Work exactly as for circular base of bird feeder.

RIM FOR LID
With 3.75mm (US size 5) needles and wire A, cast on 52 sts.
Work 3 rows in garter st.
Cast off knitwise.

BIRD
With 3mm (US size 3) needles and wire B, cast on 8 sts.
Work bird in garter st as follows:
1st–4th rows Knit.
5th row Cast on 1 st, knit to end, cast on 1 st. *(10 sts.)*
6th–8th rows Knit.
9th row Cast on 1 st, k2, yfwd, k2, [yfwd] twice, k2, yfwd, k2, cast on 1 st. *(16 sts.)*
10th row Knit.
11th row Cast on 1 st, k4, [yfwd, k2] 3 times, yfwd, k4, cast on 1 st. *(22 sts.)*
12th row Knit.
13th row Cast on 1 st, k5, yfwd, k10,

yfwd, k5, cast on 1 st. *(26 sts.)*
14th row Knit.
15th row Cast on 1 st, k6, yfwd, k12, yfwd, k6, cast on 1 st. *(30 sts.)*
16th row Knit.
17th row Cast on 1 st, k28, cast on 1 st. *(32 sts.)*
18th–20th rows Knit.
21st row K2tog, k6, k2tog, k12, k2tog, k6, k2tog. *(28 sts.)*
22nd row Knit.
23rd row K2tog, k5, k2tog, k10, k2tog, k5, k2tog. *(24 sts.)*
24th row Knit.
25th row K2tog, k4, k2tog, k8, k2tog, k4, k2tog. *(20 sts.)*
26th row [K2tog, k7] twice, k2tog. *(17 sts.)*
27th row K2tog, k5, k2tog, k6, k2tog. *(14 sts.)*
28th–30th rows Knit.
31st row K4, yfwd, k6, yfwd, k4. *(16 sts.)*
32nd row Knit.
33rd row K4, yfwd, k8, yfwd, k4. *(18 sts.)*
34th row K4, yfwd, k10, yfwd, k4. *(20 sts.)*
35th row K2tog, k3, k2tog, k6, k2tog, k3, k2tog. *(16 sts.)*
36th row K2tog, k2, k2tog, k4, k2tog, k2, k2tog. *(12 sts.)*
37th row [K2tog] twice, k4, [k2tog] twice. *(8 sts.)*
38th row [K2tog] 4 times. *(4 sts.)*
39th row K2tog twice, cut wire (leaving a long length for sewing up bird), slip end of wire through rem 2 sts, pull gently to close loop and pinch wire tog to make a point for beak.

TO FINISH
Use a blunt-ended tapestry needle and matching wire to sew all seams.

Bird feeder
Using slip stitch, sew together two side edges of main section of bird feeder to

make a tube, and sew circular base to bottom of feeder. Then cut a 30.5cm/12in length of wire A and secure it to bottom of main section of feeder opposite seam running up tube; run this length of wire through knitting around base and twist ends together to reinforce shape at base.
Cut a 28cm/11in length of wire C, weave it through top row of bird feeder to make a firm circle for lid to sit on; twist ends together to secure.
Cut a 30.5cm/12in length of wire C and loop it through seam of feeder 12.5mm/½in from cast-off edge and twist end to secure. Then curve it to make a handle, slip other end into feeder at same position on opposite side, and twist end to secure. Slip two lengths of dowelling/sticks through holes in feeder.

Bird feeder lid
Sew together cast-on and cast-off ends of rim to form a circle, and sew it to cicular lid with overcast stitch.

Bird's body
Curve bird to make correct shape (see photograph). Then starting at head, sew together two side edges using slip stitch (to form as seam running from tip of beak down centre of bird's front and belly, and to tip if underside of tail). When you reach tail, flatten it out and sew across end of tail (cast-on edge), leaving a length of wire to attach tail to lid.

Bird's feet
Cut a length of wire B about 40.5cm/16in long, fold it in half and twist it together. Slip twisted wire through belly of bird and make a V-shape at each end for feet.
Using spare wire from feet, attach bird's feet to lid, then attach tail to lid.
Fill feeder with nuts, put lid in place, hang outside, and wait for the flocks to flock.

KNITTED PETS

Cleaner, quieter, cheaper: these are just some of the
advantages of the knitted pet. Make your own tiny
fox terrier, better behaved that the real version and
almost as adorable. An obvious benefit of the knitted
ferret is that he has no teeth. Also, he won't object
to being dressed up. Ours comes with a muffler,
but see www.ferretworld.co.uk for further inspiration.
The guinea pig is very simple and comes smooth or
rough coated – just slip his coat on or off. You'll never
need to clean out his cage and he won't be eaten by
foxes. Unlike the live version, these tortoises are
extremely cheap and easy to knit and, if necessary,
you can remove the shell and wash them. You also
won't have the anxiety about tortoise rustlers.

FOX TERRIER

LEVEL

Intermediate

SIZE

The finished fox terrier measures approximately 32cm/12¹/₂in long with legs outstretched to front and back.

MATERIALS

1 x 50g/1³/₄oz ball of Rowan *Kid Classic* in main colour **MC** (off-white/Feather 829), for dog's body and legs
1 x 50g/1³/₄oz ball of Jaeger *Matchmaker Merino DK* in **A** (camel brown/Syrup 789), for markings on dog and ears
1 x 50g/1³/₄oz ball of Jaeger *Matchmaker Merino 4-Ply* in **B** (light sea blue/Mineral 741), for dog's coat
Small amount of a 4-ply-weight yarn in black, for embroidered nose and eyes
Pair of 4mm (US size 6) knitting needles
Pair of 3.25mm (US size 3) knitting needles
Toy filling
4 small white buttons, for securing legs to dog
Crochet hook, for attaching whiskers

TENSION

22 sts and 30 rows to 10cm/4in measured over st st using 4mm (US size 6) needles and MC. (**Note:** This needle size is smaller than the size recommended on the yarn label, but the fox terrier needs to be knitted tightly.)

ABBREVIATIONS

See page 17.

LEFT SIDE OF BODY

Each side of the dog's body is worked starting at the belly edge and working upwards towards the dog's spine.
With 4mm (US size 6) needles and MC, cast on 12 sts.
Beg with a k row, work 4 rows in st st, ending with a p row.

Shape belly

Cont in st st throughout and beg with a k row, cast on 6 sts at beg of next row. *(18 sts.)*
Work straight for 3 rows, ending with a p row.

Cast on 4 sts at beg of next row. *(22 sts.)*
Work straight for 5 rows, ending with a p row.
Cast on 8 sts at beg of next row. *(30 sts.)*
Work straight for 6 rows, ending with a k row.

Work marking on dog's back

Using MC and A as required, work marking on dog's back as follows:
Next row (WS) P20MC, p10A.
Next row K11A, k19MC.
Next row P18MC, p12A.
Next row K13A, k17MC.
Break off A and cont with MC only.

Shape neck

Next row (WS) P14, then turn, leaving rem 16 sts on a spare needle.
Working on these 14 sts only, cont as follows:
Dec 1 st at beg of next row and then at beg of 2 foll alt rows, ending with a k row. *(11 sts.)*
Purl 1 row.
Slip these 11 sts onto a st holder.

Shape tail

With WS facing, rejoin A to 16 sts on spare needle, cast off 10 sts purlwise (along dog's spine) and p to end. *(6 sts.)*

Working on these 6 sts only, cont as follows:
Work straight for 4 rows, ending with a p row.
Next row (RS) *K2tog, k to last st, k into front and back of last st. *(6 sts.)*
Purl 1 row.
Rep last 2 rows once more.
Work straight for 2 rows.
Cast off.

RIGHT SIDE OF BODY
With 4mm (US size 6) needles and MC, cast on 12 sts.
Beg with a k row, work 3 rows in st st, ending with a k row.

Shape belly
Cont in st st throughout and beg with a p row, cast on 6 sts at beg of next row. *(18 sts.)*
Work straight for 3 rows, ending with a k row.
Cast on 4 sts at beg of next row. *(22 sts.)*
Work straight for 5 rows, ending with a k row.
Cast on 8 sts at beg of next row. *(30 sts.)*
Work straight for 10 rows, ending with a p row.

Shape neck
Next row (RS) K14, then turn, leaving rem 16 sts on a spare needle.
Working on these 14 sts only, cont as follows:
Dec 1 st at beg of next row and then at beg of 2 foll alt rows, ending with a p row. *(11 sts.)*
Slip these 11 sts onto a second st holder and do not break off yarn.

Shape tail
With RS facing, rejoin another ball of MC to 16 sts on spare needle, cast off 10 sts (along dog's spine) and k to end. *(6 sts.)*
Working on these 6 sts only, cont as follows:
Break off MC and change to A.
Work straight for 4 rows, ending with a k row.
Next row (WS) *P2tog, p to last st,

p into front and back of last st. *(6 sts.)*
Purl 1 row.
Rep last 2 rows once more.
Work straight for 2 rows.
Cast off.

RIGHT FRONT LEG
Each leg is worked starting at foot end of leg.
With 4mm (US size 6) needles and MC, cast on 16 sts.
Beg with a k row, work 24 rows in st st, ending with a p row.
Work marking on leg
Using MC and A as required, work coloured marking on leg as follows:
Next row (RS) K13MC, k3A.
Next row P4A, p12MC.
Next row K11MC, k5A.
Next row P6A, p10MC.
Cont in st st, working 1 st more into A on each row until 34 rows st st have been worked from cast-on edge.
Cast off.

LEFT FRONT LEG
With 4mm (US size 6) needles and MC, cast on 16 sts.
Beg with a k row, work 34 rows in st st.
Cast off.

RIGHT BACK LEG
**With 4mm (US size 6) needles and MC, cast on 16 sts.
Beg with a k row, work 10 rows in st st, ending with a p row.**

Shape leg
Cont in st st throughout and beg with a k row, inc 1 st at each end of next row and then at each end of every foll k row until there are 32 sts, ending with a k row.
Work straight for 5 rows, ending with a p row.
Dec 1 st at each end of next 4 rows. *(24 sts.)*
Cast off.

LEFT BACK LEG
Work as for right back leg from ** to **.

Shape leg
Cont in st st throughout and beg with a k row, inc 1 st at each end of next row and at each end of every foll k row until there are 22 sts, ending with a k row.
Purl 1 row.
Work marking on leg
Using MC and A as required, work coloured marking on leg as follows:
Next row (RS) Using MC k into front and back of first st, k11MC, k9A, using A k into front and back of last st. *(24 sts.)*
Next row P12A, p12MC.
Next row Using MC k into front and back of first st, k12MC, k10A, using A k into front and back of last st. *(26 sts.)*
Next row P15A, p11MC.
Next row Using MC k into front and back of first st, k9MC, k15A, using A k into front and back of last st. *(28 sts.)*
Next row P18A, p10MC.
Next row Using MC k into front and back of first st, k8MC, k18A, using A k into front and back of last st. *(30 sts.)*
Next row P20A, p10MC.
Next row Using MC k into front and back of first st, k8MC, k20A, using A k into front and back of last st. *(32 sts.)*
Next row P23A, p9MC.
Break off A and cont with MC only.
Work straight for 4 rows, ending with a p row.
Dec 1 st at each end of next 4 rows. *(24 sts.)*
Cast off.

HEAD
With RS facing and using 4mm (US size 6) needles and MC (use ball of MC still attached to neck sts on right side of body), k 11 sts from holder on right side of body, then k 11 sts from holder on left side of body. *(22 sts.)*
Purl 1 row.

Shape top of head
Next row (RS) K15, pick up loop below next st on left needle by inserting tip of right needle from back to front through loop (this prevents a hole forming when turning work), then turn, leaving rem

7 sts on left needle unworked.
Work head shaping on 8 sts only as follows:
Next row P2tog (first st is loop picked up at end of last row), p7, pick up loop below next st on left needle by inserting tip of right needle from back to front through loop, then turn, leaving rem 7 sts on left needle unworked.
Next row K2tog (first st is loop picked up at end of last row), k7, pick up loop below next st on left needle, turn.
Next row P2tog (first st is loop picked up at end of last row), p7, pick up loop below next st on left needle, turn.
Rep last 2 rows twice more.
Next row K2tog (first st is loop picked up at end of last row), k7, pick up loop below next st on left needle, turn.
Next row P2tog (first st is loop picked up at end of last row), k14.
Next row K22.

Shape muzzle flap
Cast off 7 sts at beg of next 2 rows, ending with k row. (8 sts.)
Beg with a p row, work straight for 10 rows, ending with a k row.
Next row (WS) K to end, to form ridge on RS for foldline at nose.
Beg with a k row, work 5 rows in st st.
Next row (WS) K to end, to form ridge on RS for foldline at mouth.
Beg with a k row, work 8 rows in st st.
Cast off.

CHEEKS (MAKE 2)
With 4mm (US size 6) needles and MC, cast on 6 sts.
Beg with a k row, work 9 rows in st st.
Cast off.
Make second cheek in same way.

EARS (MAKE 2)
With 4mm (US size 6) needles and A, cast on 6 sts.
Beg with a k row, work 3 rows in st st, ending with a k row.
Next row (WS) K to end, to form ridge on RS for ear foldline.
Beg with a k row, work 3 rows in st st, ending with a k row.
Next row (WS) P2tog, p2, p2tog. (4 sts.)
Knit 1 row.
Next row [P2 tog] twice. (2 sts.)
Knit 1 row.

Next row P2tog, break off MC, thread tail end through rem st and pull to fasten off.
Make second ear in same way.

TOP OF DOG'S COAT
With 3.25mm (US size 3) needles and B, cast on 30 sts.
1st rib row (RS) *K2, p2; rep from * to last 2 sts, k2.
2nd rib row *P2, k2; rep from * to last 2 sts, p2.
Rep last 2 rows 4 times more, ending with a WS row (10 rows in k2, p2 rib worked from cast-on edge).

Shape coat
Cont in k2, p2 rib and taking increased sts into rib patt, inc 1 st at each end of next row and then at each end of every foll 4th row until there are 40 sts, ending with a RS row.
Work 6 rows in rib as set, ending with a RS row.

Shape neck
Next row (WS) [P2tog] 20 times. (20 sts.)
Next row [K2tog] 10 times. (10 sts.)
Break off B and leave these neck sts on a st holder.

UNDERSIDE OF DOG'S COAT
With 3.25mm (US size 3) needles and B, cast on 24 sts.
1st rib row (RS) *K1, p1; rep from * to end.
Rep last row 27 times more, ending with a WS row.

Join to top of coat
Next row (RS) Work 24 sts in k1, p1 rib as set, then with RS facing, cont in k1, p1 rib across 10 sts on st holder on top of coat. (34 sts.)

Collar
Work 8 rows more in k1, p1 rib.
Cast off in rib.

TO FINISH
Press left and right sides of body and legs lightly on wrong side, following instructions on yarn label. Do not press muzzle flap, ears or coat pieces.
Body
Sew cheeks to sides of muzzle flap, bending muzzle flap around cheeks.

Sew two sides of body together along throat, chest, belly, tail and spine, leaving an opening in chest for inserting toy filling. Insert toy filling and sew opening closed.

Legs
Fold each leg in half lengthways and sew seam along cast-on edges and side edges, leaving cast-off end open.
Insert toy filling in each leg, leaving about 1.5cm/½in at top of leg unstuffed (to allow for securing top of leg to body with a button).
Sew seam at top of each leg (cast-off edge). Sew each leg to body as shown, securing it by sewing through a button at centre of top of leg and into body.

Ears
Sew cast-on edge of each ear to head, positioning so that st st side of ear is on top and ears flop forward at foldline ridge.

Eyes and nose
Using black yarn, work two French knots for eyes and satin stitch for nose, positioning nose on nose ridge.

Whiskers
Cut two 7.5cm/3in lengths of MC. Holding lengths together, fold in half and use a crochet hook to pull looped end through a single loop on dog's head about 1cm/3⁄8in from nose and level with nose. Pull ends of yarn through loop and pull to tighten. Attach two more whisker tufts in same way close to first tuft, working away from nose.
Attach three more whisker tufts on other side of nose in same way. Trim whiskers to 1cm/3⁄8in from knots.

Coat
Sew underside of coat to top of coat along side edges, leaving an opening 2.5cm/1in long for legholes.
Dress your terrier.

FERRET

LEVEL
Intermediate

SIZE
The finished ferret measures approximately 37cm/14½in long from mouth to tip of tail.

MATERIALS
1 x 50g/1¾oz ball of Rowan *Pure Wool DK* or Jaeger *Matchmaker Merino DK* in main colour **MC** (rust), for top side of ferret's body and head
1 x 50g/1¾oz ball of Rowan *Pure Wool DK* or Jaeger *Matchmaker Merino DK* in contrasting colour **A** (dark brown), for tail, legs and ears
1 x 50g/1¾oz ball of Rowan *Pure Wool DK* or Jaeger *Matchmaker Merino DK* in contrasting colour **B** (off-white), for claws and underside of ferret's body and head
1 x 50g/1¾oz ball of Rowan *4-Ply Soft* or Jaeger *Matchmaker Merino 4-Ply* in contrasting colour **C** (dusky lilac), for scarf
Small amount of double-knitting weight yarn in black, for embroidered nose
Pair of 4mm (US size 6) knitting needles
Pair of 3.25mm (US size 3) knitting needles
Toy filling
2 small black buttons, for eyes

TENSION
22 sts and 30 rows to 10cm/4in measured over st st using 4mm (US size 6) needles and MC.

ABBREVIATIONS
See page 17.

TAIL AND TOP OF BODY AND HEAD
This section is worked starting at the tail.

Shape tail
With 4mm (US size 6) needles and A, cast on 1 st.
1st row K into front and back of st. *(2 sts.)*
2nd row P to end.
Cont in st st throughout and beg with a k row, inc 1 st at each end of next row and then at each end every alt row 5 times, ending with a k row. *(14 sts.)*
Purl 1 row.

Inc 1 st each end of next row and each end of every foll 4th row until there are 28 sts.
Cont in st st throughout, work until tail measures 15cm/6in from cast-on edge, ending with a p row.
Next row (RS) [K3tog] 9 times, k1. *(10 sts.)*

Begin body
Break off A and change to MC.
Inc 1 st at each end of next 2 rows. *(14 sts.)*
Purl 1 row.
**Next row (RS) K into front and back of first st, k2, k into front and back of next

st, k to last 4 sts, k into front and back of next st, k2, k into front and back of last st.
Purl 1 row.**
Rep from ** to ** 3 times more. *(30 sts.)*
Work straight until work measures 7cm/ 3in from beginning of body, ending with a p row.

Shape humpback
Next row (RS) K26, pick up loop below next st on left needle by inserting tip of right needle from back to front through loop (this prevents a hole forming when turning work), then turn, leaving rem

4 sts on left needle unworked.
Work hump on 22 sts only as follows:
Next row P2tog (first st is loop picked up at end of last row), p21, pick up loop below next st on left needle by inserting tip of right needle from back to front through loop, then turn, leaving rem 4 sts on left needle unworked.
Next row K2tog (first st is loop picked up at end of last row), k21, pick up loop below next st on left needle, turn.
Next row P2tog (first st is loop picked up at end of last row), p21, pick up loop below next st on left needle, turn.
Rep last 2 rows once more.
Next row K2tog (first st is loop picked up at end of last row), k25.
Next row P30.
Work straight for 6 rows, ending with a p row.

Shape neck
Dec 1 st at each end of next row. *(28 sts.)*
Work straight for 3 rows, ending with a p row.
Dec 1 st at each end of next row. *(26 sts.)*
Purl 1 row.
Next row** K2tog, k2, k2tog, k to last 6 sts, k2tog, k2, k2tog. *(22 sts.)*
Work straight for 3 rows, ending with a p row.
Rep from *** to *** once. *(18 sts.)*
Work straight for 9 rows, ending with a p row.

Shape head
Next row (RS) K15, pick up loop below next st on left needle, then turn, leaving rem 3 sts on left needle unworked.
Work head shaping on 12 sts only as follows:
Next row P2tog (first st is loop picked up at end of last row), p11, pick up loop below next st on left needle, then turn, leaving rem 3 sts on left needle unworked.
Next row K2tog (first st is loop picked up at end of last row), k11, pick up loop below next st on left needle, turn.
Next row P2tog (first st is loop picked up at end of last row), p11, pick up loop below next st on left needle, turn.
Rep last 2 rows once more.
Next row K2tog (first st is loop picked up at end of last row), k14.
Next row P18.

Shape muzzle
Next row (RS) K6, then turn, leaving rem 12 sts unworked.
Working on these 6 sts only, cont as follows:
Purl 1 row.
Next row K2tog, k4. *(5 sts.)*
Purl 1 row.
Next row K2tog, k3. *(4 sts.)*
Purl 1 row.
Next row K2tog, k2. *(3 sts.)*
Purl 1 row.
Next row K2tog, k1. *(2 sts.)*
Next row P2tog, break off MC and fasten off.
With RS facing, rejoin MC to rem 12 sts, k 6 centre sts, then turn, leaving rem 6 sts unworked.
Working on these 6 centre sts only, cont as follows:
Purl 1 row.
Next row K2tog, k2, k2tog. *(4 sts.)*
Next row P2tog, p2tog. *(2 sts.)*
Next row K2tog, break off MC and fasten off.
With RS facing, rejoin MC to rem 6 sts and k to end.
Purl 1 row.
Next row K4, k2tog. *(5 sts.)*
Purl 1 row.
Next row K3, k2tog. *(4 sts.)*
Purl 1 row.
Next row K2, k2tog. *(3 sts.)*
Purl 1 row.
Next row K1, k2tog. *(2 sts.)*
Next row P2tog, break off MC and fasten off.

UNDERSIDE OF BODY AND HEAD
This section is worked starting at the head.

Shape underside of mouth and neck
With 4mm needles and B, cast on 2 sts.
1st row (RS) K into front and back of each st. *(4 sts.)*
Cont in st st throughout and beg with a p row, work straight for 3 rows, ending with a p row.
Inc 1 st at each end of next row. *(6 sts.)*
Work straight for 7 rows, ending with a p row.
Inc 1 st at each end of next row. *(8 sts.)*
Work straight for 11 rows, ending with a p row.
Inc 1 st at each end of next row. *(10 sts.)*
Work straight for 5 rows, ending with a p row.
Inc 1 st at each end of next row. *(12 sts.)*

Work straight for 25 rows, ending with a p row.
Dec 1 st at each end of next row and then at each end of every alt row 3 times, ending with a k row. *(4 sts.)*
Purl 1 row.
Next row [K2tog] twice.
Purl 1 row.
Next row K2tog, break off B and fasten off.

EARS (MAKE 2)
With 4mm (US size 6) needles and A, cast on 7 sts.
Beg with a k row, work 3 rows in st st, ending with a k row.
Cast off knitwise.
Make second ear in same way.

FRONT LEGS (MAKE 2)
The front legs are worked starting at the top of the leg.

Shape leg
With 4mm (US size 6) needles and A, cast on 20 sts.
Beg with a k row, work 6 rows in st st, ending with a p row.
****Next row (RS)** K2tog, k to last 2 sts, k2tog.
Purl 1 row.
Rep last 2 rows 3 times more. *(12 sts.)*

Shape heel
Next row (RS) K9, pick up loop below next st on left needle, then turn, leaving rem 3 sts on left needle unworked.
Work heel shaping on 6 sts only as follows:
Next row P2tog (first st is loop picked up at end of last row), p5, pick up loop below next st on left needle, then turn, leaving rem 3 sts on left needle unworked.
Next row K2tog (first st is loop picked up at end of last row), k5, pick up loop below next st on left needle, turn.
Next row P2tog (first st is loop picked up at end of last row), p5, pick up loop below next st on left needle, turn.
Rep last 2 rows once more.
Next row K2tog (first st is loop picked up at end of last row), k8.
Mark each end of last row with a piece of coloured thread.

Shape foot
Next row P2tog, p8, p2tog. *(10 sts.)*
Next row K2tog, k6, k2tog. *(8 sts.)*

Next row P2tog, p4, p2tog. *(6 sts.)*
Next row K2tog, k2, k2tog. *(4 sts.)*
Next row [P2tog] twice. *(2 sts.)*
Next row K2tog, break off A and fasten off.
Make second leg in same way.

BACK LEGS (MAKE 2)
The back legs are worked starting at the
top of the leg.

Shape leg
With 4mm (US size 6) needles and A,
cast on 20 sts.
Beg with a k row, work 4 rows in st st,
ending with a p row. Complete as for front
legs from ****.
Make second leg in same way.

SCARF
With 3.25mm (US size 3) needles and C,
cast on 8 sts.
Work in garter st (knit every row) until
the scarf measures 28cm/11in from the
cast-on edge. Cast off knitwise.

TO FINISH
Do not press pieces.
Muzzle
Sew the two muzzle seams to join sides
of muzzle to centre section, easing in
side sections.

Body
Sew underside of body and head to top of
body and head, leaving an opening in
seam for inserting toy filling. Insert toy filling
in body and sew opening closed.

Tail
Sew side edges of tail together. (Do not
insert toy filling in tail.)

Ears
Sew cast-on edge of ears to top of head as
shown (above head shaping turning rows),
gathering edge slightly and positioning so
that ears curl downwards and rev st st side
is on top.

Legs
Sew together side edges of one front
leg, stitching from cast-on edge to markers
so that foot is left open.
Sew seams on three remaining legs in
same way.
Insert toy filling in each leg, then pinch
together top of leg (cast-on edge) and sew
so that leg seam is at one end of top seam.
Sew short back legs to seam lines between
top and underside of ferret (one on each
side), about 1.5cm/½in from tail. Sew
long front legs to same seam line and about
7cm/2¾in in front of back legs.
Using B, embroider three short stitches
around front of each foot for claws as shown
in photograph.

Eyes and nose
Sew on buttons for eyes.
Embroider nose with black yarn.
Tie scarf around neck.

GUINEA PIG

LEVEL
Easy

SIZE
The finished guinea pig measures approximately 20.5cm/8in long.

MATERIALS
1 x 50g/1³/₄oz ball of Rowan *Kid Classic* in main colour **MC** (charcoal/ Smoke 831), for guinea pig
Small amount of Rowan *Kid Classic* in contrasting colour **A** (pale pink/ Sherbet Dip 850), for embroidered feet, mouth and nose
1 x 25g/⁷/₈oz ball of Rowan *Kidsilk Haze* in contrasting colour **B** (light brown), for coat
Pair of 4mm (US size 6) knitting needles
Pair of 5mm (US size 8) knitting needles
Toy filling
2 small buttons, for eyes

TENSION
Body: 22 sts and 30 rows to 10cm/ 4in measured over st st using 4mm (US size 6) needles and MC.
(**Note:** This needle size is smaller than recommended on the yarn label, but the guinea pig must be knitted tightly.)
Coat: 18 sts and 27 rows to 10cm/ 4in measured over loopy stitch using 5mm (US size 8) needles and B.

ABBREVIATIONS
See page 17.

TOP OF BODY
With 4mm (US size 6) needles and MC, cast on 12 sts (head end of toy).
Beg with a k row, work in st st, inc 1 st at each end of first 4 rows, ending with a p row. *(20 sts.)*
Cont in st st throughout and beg with a k row, work straight for 6 rows, ending with a p row.
Inc 1 st at each end of next row. *(22 sts.)*
St st for 7 rows, ending with a p row.
Inc 1 st at each end of next row. *(24 sts.)*
Work straight until work measures 18cm/7in from cast-on edge, ending with a p row.
Dec 1 st at each end of next 8 rows, ending with a p row. *(8 sts.)*
Cast off.

UNDERSIDE OF BODY
Make exactly as for top of body.

EARS (MAKE 2)
With 4mm (US size 6) needles and MC, cast on 6 sts.
1st row (RS) K to end.
2nd row P to end.
3rd row K2tog, k2, k2tog. *(4 sts.)*
4th row [P2tog] twice.
5th row K2tog, break off MC, thread tail end through rem st and pull to fasten off.
Make second ear in same way.

GUINEA PIG'S COAT
With 5mm (US size 8) needles and B, cast on 36 sts.
1st–4th rows K to end.
Work 2cm (³/₄in) loop stitches (see page 13) on next row as follows:
5th row (WS) Place first finger of left hand behind first st on left needle, then wrap yarn around this finger and right needle at same time and k first st, do not drop st off left needle but slip st on right needle back onto left needle while keeping finger inside loop, k2tog tbl (to work slipped st and next st on left needle tog) and slide finger out of loop to complete first loop st, *wrapping yarn around first finger of left hand as before to create a loop, knit next st without dropping st from left needle, slip st just made back onto left needle and k2tog tbl; rep from * to end. *(36 sts.)*
6th row K each st tbl.
Rep 1st–6th rows 3 times more.
Knit 1 row.
Next row Cast on 6 sts onto left needle, k to end.
Rep last row once more. Cast off knitwise.

TO FINISH
Very lightly press top and underside of body on wrong side, following instructions on yarn label. Do not press coat. With right sides together, sew top of body to underside of body, leaving a small opening. Turn right side out and insert toy filling until guinea pig is firmly filled. Sew opening closed. Sew one side edge of each ear to head as shown. (**Note:** If desired, position seam along centre back of toy.)

Nose, mouth, feet and eyes
Using A (or scrap of black yarn), embroider nose and mouth as shown. Using A, embroider feet on underside of body as shown (**Fig 1**). Sew on buttons for eyes.

Coat
Sew two ends of coat cast-off row together. Slip coat over guinea pig's head.

①

TORTOISE

SIZE

The finished tortoise measures approximately 16.5cm/6½in long from mouth to tip of tail and 13.5cm/5¼in wide across back legs.

MATERIALS

1 x 50g/1¾oz ball of Jaeger *Matchmaker Merino 4-Ply* in main colour **MC**, for tortoise's body

1 x 50g/1¾oz ball of Rowan *Pure Wool DK* in a contrasting colour **A**, for tortoise's shell

Pair of 4mm (US size 6) knitting needles

Pair of 3.25mm (US size 3) knitting needles

Cable needle

Toy filling

TENSION

Tortoise's body: 28 sts and 36 rows to 10cm/4in measured over st st using 3.25mm (US size 3) needles and MC.

Tortoise's shell: 22 sts and 30 rows to 10cm/4in measured over st st using 4mm (US size 6) needles and A.

ABBREVIATIONS

T4LF (twist 4 left) = slip next st onto cable needle and hold at front of work, p3, then k1 from cable needle.

T4RB (twist 4 right) = slip next 3 sts onto cable needle and hold at back of work, k1, then p3 from cable needle.

Also see page 17.

TORTOISE'S BODY

The top and bottom of the tortoise's body are worked in one piece in st st, starting at the tail of the top of the body.

Shape tail

With 3.25mm (US size 3) needles and MC, cast on 1 st.

1st row (RS) K into front and back of st. *(2 sts.)*

2nd row P to end.

3rd row K into front and back of each st. *(4 sts.)*

4th row P to end.

Cont in st st throughout and beg with a k row, inc 1 st at each end of next 5 rows, ending with a k row. *(14 sts.)*

Purl 1 row.

Shape back legs

Cast on 12 sts at beg of next 2 rows. *(38 sts.)*

Work straight for 5 rows, ending with a k row.

Cast off 8 sts at beg of next 2 rows. *(22 sts.)*

Work straight for 18 rows, ending with a k row.

Shape front legs

Cast on 8 sts at beg of next 2 rows. *(38 sts.)*

Work straight for 5 rows, ending with a p row.

Cast off 12 sts at beg of next 2 rows. *(14 sts.)*

Shape neck and head

Next row (RS) [K2tog, k2] 3 times, k2tog. *(10 sts.)*

Purl 1 row.

Next row (RS) K2tog, k6, k2tog. *(8 sts.)*

Purl 1 row.

Inc 1 st at each end of next row. *(10 sts.)*
Work straight for 3 rows, ending with
a p row.
**Dec 1 st at each end of next row.
Work straight for 1 row.**
Rep from ** to ** once, ending with
a p row. *(6 sts.)*
Next row (RS) P to end, to create ridge
for mouth.
This completes top of tortoise's body.
Work bottom of tortoise's body as follows:

Shape neck and head
Purl 1 row.
Beg with a k row and cont in st st, inc 1 st
at each end of next row. *(8 sts.)*
Purl 1 row.
Inc 1 st at each end of next row. *(10 sts.)*
Work straight for 3 rows, ending with
a p row.
Dec 1 st at each end of next row. *(8 sts.)*
Purl 1 row.
Inc 1 st at each end of next row. *(10 sts.)*
Purl 1 row.
Next row (RS) K into front and back of
first st, [k2, k into front and back of next st]
3 times. *(14 sts.)*

Shape front legs
Cast on 12 sts at beg of next 2 rows.
(38 sts.)
Work straight for 5 rows, ending with
a p row.
Cast off 8 sts at beg of next 2 rows.
(22 sts.)
Work straight for 19 rows, ending with
a k row.

Shape back legs
Cast on 8 sts, at beg of next 2 rows.
(38 sts.)
Work straight for 5 rows, ending with
a p row.
Cast off 12 sts at beg of next 2 rows.
(14 sts.)

Shape tail
Dec 1 st at each end of next row and then
at each end of 5 foll alt rows, ending with
a k row. *(2 sts.)*
Next row (WS) P2tog, then break off A,
thread tail end through rem st and pull to
fasten off.

TOP OF TORTOISE'S SHELL
The top of the tortoise's shell is worked
starting at the neck end.
With 4mm (US size 6) needles and A,
cast on 26 sts.
Work 2 rows in garter st (knit every row).
Work turtle check patt as follows:
1st row (RS) K4, p6, k6, p6, k4.
2nd row P4, k6, p6, k6, p4.
3rd row K3, T4LF, T4RB, k4, T4LF,
T4RB, k3.
4th row P3, k3, p2, k3, p4, k3, p2,
k3, p3.
5th row K2, [T4LF, k2, T4RB, k2] twice.
6th row P2, [k3, p4, k3, p2] twice.
7th row K1, [T4LF, k4, T4RB] twice, k1.
8th row (inc row) K into front and back
of first st, k3, p6, k6, p6, k3, k into front
and back of last st. *(28 sts.)*
9th row P5, k6, p6, k6, p5.
10th row (inc row) K into front and back
of first st, k4, p6, k6, p6, k4, k into front
and back of last st. *(30 sts.)*
11th row [P6, k6] twice, p6.
12th row [K6, p6] twice, k6.
13th row K3, [T4RB, k4, T4LF] twice, k3.
14th row (inc row) P into front and back
of first st, p3, [k3, p4, k3, p2] twice, p1,
p into front and back of last st. *(32 sts.)*
15th row K5, [T4RB, k2, T4LF, k2] twice, k3.
16th row P6, k3, p2, k3, p4, k3, p2,
k3, p6.
17th row K6, T4RB, T4LF, k4, T4RB,
T4LF, k6.
18th row P7, k6, p6, k6, p7.
19th row K7, p6, k6, p6, k7.
20th and 21st rows Rep 18th and
19th rows.
22nd row Rep 20th row.
23rd row K6, T4LF, T4RB, k4,T4LF,
T4RB, k6.
24th row P6, k3, p2, k3, p4, k3,
p2, k3, p6.
25th row K5, [T4LF, k2, T4RB, k2]
twice, k3.
26th row P5, [k3, p4, k3, p2] twice, p3.
27th row K4, [T4LF, k4, T4RB] twice, k4.
28th row (inc row) K into front and
back of first st, [k6, p6] twice, k6,
k into front and back of last st. *(34 sts.)*
29th row P8, k6, p6, k6, p8.
30th row (inc row) K into front and
back of first st, k7, p6, k6, p6, k7,
k into front and back of last st. *(36 sts.)*

31st row P9, k6, p6, k6, p9.
32nd row K9, p6, k6, p6, k9.
33rd row Cast off first 6 sts knitwise,
k to end. *(30 sts.)*
34th row Rep 33rd row. *(24 sts.)*
K 1 row.
Cast off knitwise.

UNDERSIDE OF TORTOISE'S SHELL
The underside of the tortoise's shell is
worked starting at the tail end of the shell.
With 4mm (US size 6) needles and A,
cast on 20 sts.
Work 22 rows in garter st.

Shape legholes
Cont in garter st throughout, cast off 4 sts
at beg of next 2 rows.
Work straight for 6 rows.
Cast off.

TO FINISH
Do not press.

Body
Fold tortoise's body in half at ridge row
(mouth), with right sides together. Sew
seam around edge of body, leaving an
opening in seam between two legs on one
side of body. Turn tortoise right side out.
Insert toy filling – do not overstuff, as the
tortoise should be fairly flat and floppy.
Sew opening closed.

Eyes
For each of tortoise's eyes, work two short
stitches on top of each other using A.

Shell
Lay shell top wrong side up and place
underside of shell right side up on top
of it; position underside so that its cast-on
edge is about 2cm/^{3}/4in from cast-off
edge of shell top. Pin underside in place
so that shell top will create a 0.5cm/^{1}/2in
overhang over it along side edges and a
6mm/^{1}/4in overhang at shoulders. Sew
two corners on cast-off edge of underside
to shell top to form shoulders, leaving an
opening for tortoise's head. Starting at
cast-on end of underside, sew sides of
underside to shell top, leaving last 6 rows
of underside open for tortoise's front legs.
Pop tortoise inside its shell.

CHARTS

Carrot Curtain
(page 29)

KEY
■ p on RS and k on WS using **MC**
■ k on RS and p on WS using **A**

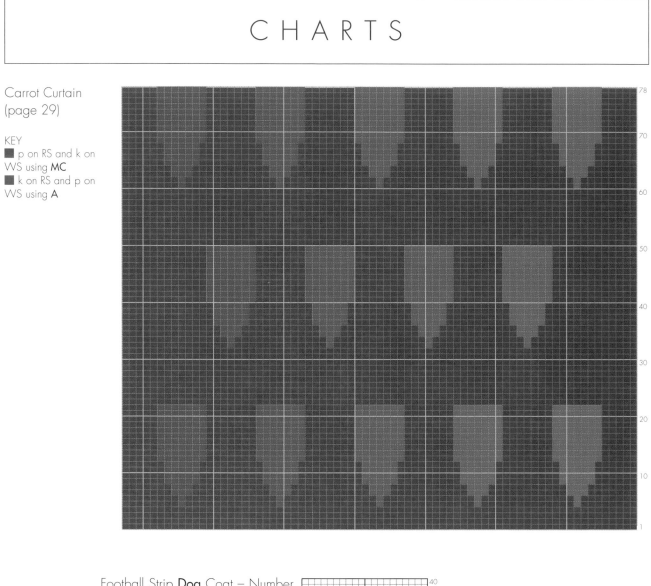

Football Strip **Dog** Coat – Number
(page 33/34)

Football Strip **Dog** Coat – Badge
(page 34)

KEY
■ MC
☐ A

Spot **Dog** Coat (page 39)

24-row repeat

36 30 20 13 10

large

extra small

extra small

large

24-row repeat

36 30 20 13 10

extra large

medium

small

small

medium

extra large

KEY
MC
Spot Motif

Floral **Dog** Coat
(page 42)

KEY
MC
A
B
C
D

150 140 130 120 110 100 90 80 70

128

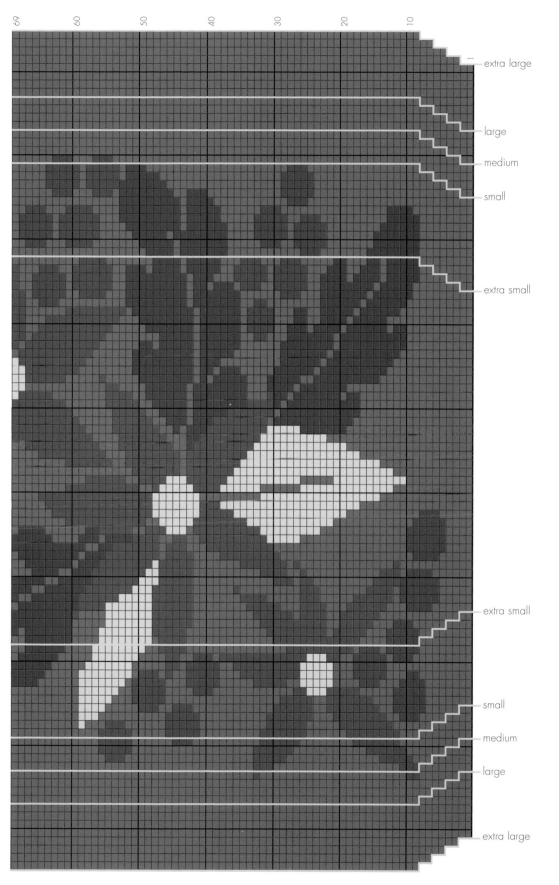

69　　　60　　　50　　　40　　　30　　　20　　　10

— extra large

— large

— medium

— small

— extra small

— extra small

— small

— medium

— large

— extra large

129

Baroque **Cat** Cushion
(page 47)

KEY
■ MC
■ A

Heraldic **Cat** Cushion
(page 49)

KEY

■ MC
■ A
■ B
■ C

Horse Blanket – Square 1
(page 56)

KEY

■ M
■ E

Horse Blanket – Square 3
(page 56)

KEY
■ D
■ L

Horse Blanket – Square 6
(page 57)

KEY

■ A
■ C

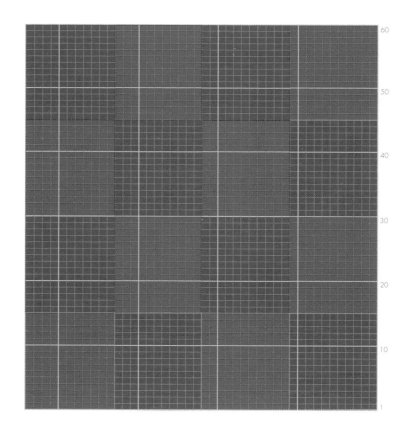

Horse Blanket – Square 8
(page 57)

KEY

■ G
■ J
■ L

Horse Blanket – Square 9
(page 57)

KEY

■ A
■ K

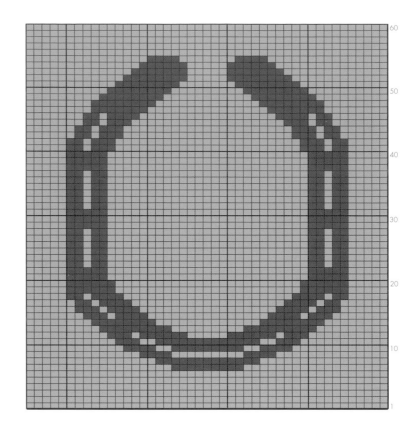

Horse Blanket – Square 14
(page 57)

KEY

■ G
■ K

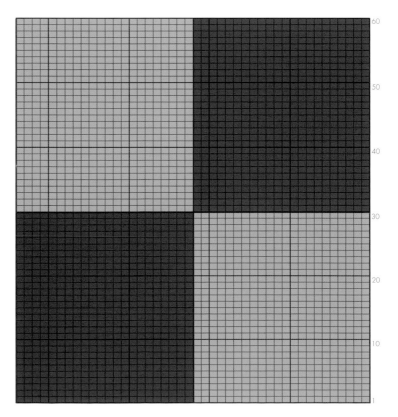

Horse Blanket – Square 15
(page 57)

KEY
 J
■ L

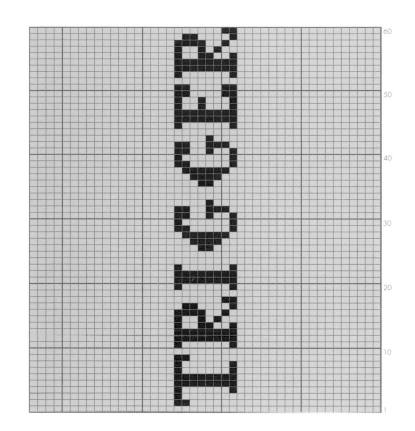

Horse Blanket – Square 17
(page 57)

KEY
 G
■ H

Spot **Dog** Collar
(page 67)

KEY
□ MC
■ Spot Motif

Hell's Angel **Dog** Collar
(page 68)

KEY
■ MC
■ A
□ B
■ C

Floral **Dog** Collar
(page 66)

KEY
■ MC
■ A
■ B
■ C
■ D

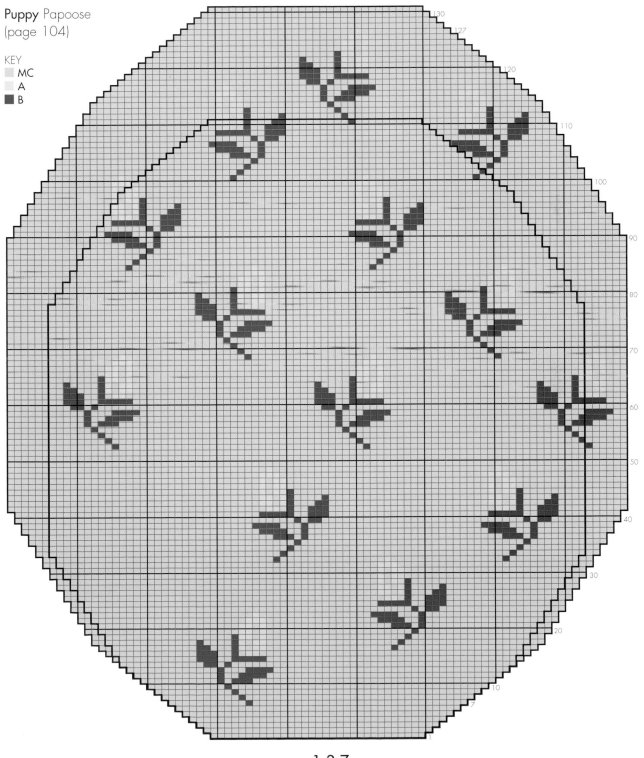

Puppy Papoose
(page 104)

KEY
MC
A
B

137

Budgie Blanket
(page 85)

KEY
MC
A
B
C
D
E
F

YARN INFORMATION

The yarns used in this book are listed below. Yarn manufacturers change their yarn colours often, so we cannot guarantee that the yarn colours specified in some of the patterns will still be available when you come to use this book. Similar shades can be used instead, or you can use your leftover yarns in your chosen colour combinations.

If you wish to use a substitute yarn, be sure to look for a yarn that is similar in weight and texture and calculate the amount you need by the length of the ball rather than by the weight. The descriptions given here for the yarns will help you identify a similar yarn for substitution.

To obtain these yarns, look up the websites below to find a mail-order stockist or store in your area:
www.angelyarns.com
www.debbieblissonline.com
www.knitrowan.com
www.yeoman-yarns.co.uk

ROWAN YARNS

Rowan *Cotton Glace*
A fine-weight 100% cotton yarn
Recommended tension: 23 sts and 32 rows to 10cm/4in measured over st st using 3.25–3.75mm (US size 3–5) knitting needles
Ball size: Approximately 15m/126yd per 50g/1$\frac{3}{4}$oz ball

Rowan *Felted Tweed*
A lightweight wool-mix yarn
Yarn specification: 50% merino wool, 25% alpaca, 25% viscose
Recommended tension: 22–24 sts and 30–32 rows to 10cm/4in measured over st st using 3.75–4mm (US size 5–6) knitting needles
Ball size: Approximately 175m/191yd per 50g/1$\frac{3}{4}$oz ball

Rowan *4-Ply Soft*
A super-fine-weight 100% merino wool yarn
Recommended tension: 28 sts and 36 rows to 10cm/4in measured over st st using 3.25mm (US size 3) knitting needles

Ball size: Approximately 175m/191yd per 50g/1$\frac{3}{4}$oz ball

Rowan *Kid Classic*
A medium-weight mohair-mix yarn
Yarn specification: 70% lambswool, 26% kid mohair, 4% nylon
Recommended tension: 18–19 sts and 23–25 rows to 10cm/4in measured over st st using 5–5.5mm (US size 8–9) knitting needles
Ball size: Approximately 140m/153yd per 50g/1$\frac{3}{4}$oz ball

Rowan *Kidsilk Haze*
A fine-weight mohair-silk-mix yarn
Yarn specification: 70% super kid mohair, 30% silk
Recommended tension: 18–25 sts and 23–34 rows to 10cm/4in measured over st st using 3.25–5mm (US size 3–8) knitting needles
Ball size: Approximately 210m/229yd per 25g/$\frac{7}{8}$oz ball

Rowan *Pure Wool DK*
A lightweight 100% super-wash wool yarn
Recommended tension: 22 sts and 30 rows to 10cm/4in measured over st st using 4mm (US size 6) knitting needles
Ball size: Approximately 125m/137yd per 50g/1$\frac{3}{4}$oz ball

Rowan *Scottish Tweed Aran*
A medium-weight 100% pure wool yarn
Recommended tension: 16 sts and 23 rows to 10cm/4in measured over st st using 5–5.5mm (US size 8–9) knitting needles
Ball size: Approximately 170m/186yd per 100g/3$\frac{1}{2}$oz ball

Rowan *Scottish Tweed Chunky*
A chunky-weight 100% pure wool yarn
Recommended tension: 12 sts and 16 rows to 10cm/4in measured over st st using 8mm (US size 11) knitting needles
Ball size: Approximately 100m/109yd per 100g/3$\frac{1}{2}$oz ball

Rowan *Scottish Tweed 4-Ply*
A fine-weight 100% pure wool yarn
Recommended tension: 26–28 sts and 38–40 rows to 10cm/4in measured over st st using 3–3.25mm (US size 3) knitting needles
Ball size: Approximately 110m/120yd per 25g/$\frac{7}{8}$oz ball

JAEGER YARNS

Jaeger *Fur*
A super-chunky-weight mohair-mix yarn
Yarn specification: 47% kid mohair, 47% wool, 6% polymide
Recommended tension: 8 sts and 9 rows to 10cm/4in measured over st st using 10mm (US size 15) knitting needles
Ball size: Approximately 20m/22yd per 50g/1$\frac{3}{4}$oz ball

Jaeger *Matchmaker Merino DK*
A lightweight 100% merino wool yarn (machine washable)
Recommended tension: 22 sts and 30 rows to 10cm/4in measured over st st using 4mm (US size 6) knitting needles
Ball size: Approximately 120m/131yd per 50g/1$\frac{3}{4}$oz ball

Jaeger *Matchmaker Merino 4-Ply*
A super-fine-weight 100% merino wool yarn (machine washable)
Recommended tension: 28 sts and 36 rows to 10cm/4in measured over st st using 3.25mm (US size 3) knitting needles
Ball size: Approximately 183m/200yd per 50g/1$\frac{3}{4}$oz ball

TWILLEYS YARNS

Twilleys *Goldfingering*
A super-fine-weight metallic-mix yarn
Yarn specification: 80% viscose, 20% metallised polyester
Recommended tension: 28 sts and 36 rows to 10cm/4in measured over st st using 3-3.25mm (US size 3) knitting needles
Ball size: Approximately 100m/108yd per 25g/$\frac{7}{8}$oz per ball

STOCKISTS

Most of the materials used in this book are available from good local craft shops or try:

Creative Beadcraft
20 Beak Street
London
W1F 9RE
Tel 44 (0)20 7777629 9964
Mail order 44 (0)1494 778818
www.creativebeadcraft.co.uk

John Lewis
Oxford Street
London W1A 1EX
Tel 020 7629 7711
www.johnlewis.com

Polystyrene balls for the beanbag filling and cushion pads for cat cushions.

MacCulloch & Wallis
25–26 Dering Street
London
W1S 1AT
Tel 020 7629 0311
www.macculloch-wallis.co.uk

Calico for the beanbag cushion, striped mattress ticking and polyester Double Satin Ribbon 50mm/5cm wide for the Puppy Papoose.

Muir and Osborne
33 Sillwood Rd
Brighton
BN1 2LE
Tel 44 (0)1273736106
www.petheaven.org.uk

Some of the accessories are available ready-made through our website

The Bead Shop
21a Tower Street
London
WC2H 9NS
Tel 44 (0)20 7240 0931
Mail order 44 (0)20 8553 3240
www.beadshop.co.uk

Shops and mail order in America trading under 'Beadworks'

The Bead Shop
21 Sydney Street
Brighton
BN1 4EN
Tel 44 (0)1273 675077
Mail order 44 (0)1273 740777
www.beadsunlimited.co.uk

Sew-on jewels for Eco-Dog Coats, fake pearls or any beads

ACKNOWLEDGEMENTS

A book like this cannot happen overnight; we have been working on it for many months. We would like to thank our friends and families: Orlando, Daniel, Milo, Geoffrey, Abigail, Gabriel. They have all been extremely helpful both with suggestions and with tactful reactions to our ideas.

We would also like to thank all our dogs past and present who have been highly involved in our knitwear business: Alice, Fanny, Dorothy, Jack Swan, Nell and Lily. Nell, a lovely whippet lurcher, has been the house model for the dog coats and Lily has helped in her own way.

Our wonderful and expert knitters who have worked on the patterns and tolerate demands most people wouldn't: Mrs Allday, Karen Cleverley, Kay Jones, Rosemary Moore, Mrs Saunders, Sheila Self, Jennifer Smith, Sylvia Smith, Norma Stent, Pauline Taylor, Sheila Taylor, Eileen Trudgeon, and Paula and the Stitch and Bitch group in Frome. We must also mention all the other people, who over many years have supported us with their magnificent knitting.

Thank you to Rowan Yarns for their generosity. We are extremely grateful for the meticulous pattern checking by Marilyn Wilson and Sally Harding. Many thanks to Caroline Dawnay and Jean Edelstein for all their encouragement, and for putting us together with Quadrille.

Enormous gratitude to Jane O'Shea, Laura Herring, Katherine Case, Helen Lewis and everyone at Quadrille who have worked with such enthusiasm on this book and who put us together with the brilliant Diana Miller. Her photographs have exceeded all our expectations.

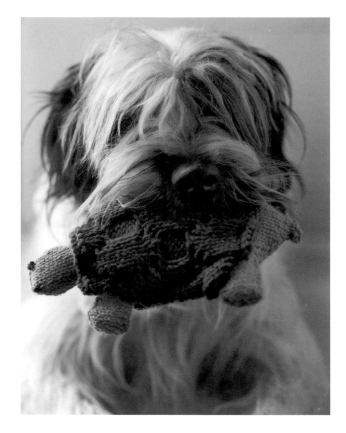

A big thank you to all the models and animals who helped in the making of this book:

Biddy
Big Red
Charlie, the spaniel
Charlie, the terrier
Dave
Dolly and Edith
Feisty
Fred
Georgie
Grace
Ho Chi
Jake
Joey
Katie
Larry
Lila
Lily, the Whippet
Lily and Gus, the Pugs
Loulou
Matthew
Mooli
Mr Q

Mrs Mimsy
Nell
Neville
Oristano
Patch
Reggie
Ronnie
Rufus
Saint Godegrand
Sydney
Taz
Violet
Wilf

With thanks to Milton Harries for the race horses.

Many thanks to Hackney City Farm.

And in loving memory of Sandy and Burt, R.I.P.